LONGMAN

CORNERSTONE

C

Practice Book

Anna Uhl Chamot

Jim Cummins

Sharroky Hollie

PEARSON
Longman

Longman Cornerstone C
Practice Book

Pearson Education, 10 Bank Street, White Plains, NY 10606

Staff credits: The people who made up the *Longman Cornerstone* team, representing editorial, production, design, manufacturing, and marketing, are John Ade, Rhea Banker, Liz Barker, Kenna Bourke, Jeffrey Buckner, Brandon Carda, Daniel Comstock, Martina Deignan, Gina DiLillo, Nancy Flaggman, Cate Foley, Patrice Fraccio, Tracy Grenier, Zach Halper, Henry Hild, Sarah Hughes, Karen Kawaguchi, Lucille Kennedy, Ed Lamprich, Jamie Lawrence, Niki Lee, Christopher Leonowicz, Tara Maceyak, Katrinka Moore, Linda Moser, Liza Pleva, Edie Pullman, Monica Rodriguez, Tara Rose, Tania Saiz-Sousa, Chris Siley, Heather St. Clair, Loretta Steeves, and Andrew Vaccaro.
Text composition: The Quarasan Group, Inc.

ISBN-13: 978-0-13-235691-6
ISBN-10: 0-13-235691-0

PEARSON LONGMAN ON THE **WEB**

Pearsonlongman.com offers online resources for teachers and students. Access our Companion Websites, our online catalog, and our local offices around the world.

Visit us at **www.pearsonlongman.com**.

Printed in the United States of America

13 14 15 16—V016—14 13 12

CONTENTS

CONTENTS

Name _____ Date _____

Vocabulary

Use with Student Book pages 8–9.

Key Words

- ~~important~~ ✓
- ~~complete~~
- ~~exclaimed~~
- ~~clumsy~~ ✓
- ~~improve~~ ✓
- ~~suspicious~~

A. Choose the word that *best* completes each sentence. Write the word.

1. The waiter dropped the food because

   he was _Clumsy_.

2. Make sure you _complete_ every question on the test.

3. You can _improve_ if you practice every day.

4. The teacher was _suspicious_ when he found all the students' test answers were the same.

5. "You're the best!" Casey _exclaimed_.

6. We have an _important_ game on Saturday.

B. Choose the word that *best* matches the meaning of the underlined words. Write the word.

7. Players <u>get better</u> when they play every day.

   Improve

8. Don't be <u>distrustful</u> of people trying to help!

   Suspicious

9. It's <u>necessary and means a lot</u> to follow the rules.

   important

10. I broke everything because I'm really <u>uncoordinated</u>.

    Clumsy

C. Answer the questions.

11. What things do you like to **complete**?

I like to complete math problems.

12. How can an athlete **improve** his or her game?

An athlete can improve by practicing.

13. What was the message the team **exclaimed** when they won?

The team exclaimed, "We Won! played fair."

14. When have you been **clumsy**?

I've been clumsy when I spilled water everywhere.

15. Why is it **important** to do your homework?

It's important to do your homework so you don't get a 0 or lose a recess.

16. When have you been **suspicious**?

When I finished a test really fast.

Academic Words

D. Read each sentence. Write a new sentence using the underlined word.

17. The audience watched the music director <u>conduct</u> the orchestra.

I conduct the class every day.

18. The students made a model for their science <u>project</u>.

I made a project for my class.

 Home-School Connection Write a sentence for each key word. Share your sentences with a family member.

Name _____   Date _____

Reader's Companion
Use with Student Book pages 10–15.

Everybody Wins

For the next three weeks, Jessie helped Casey with her science homework.

"When you study," Jessie told Casey, "first read the chapter all the way through. Then go back and write down the words you don't know. You can look up these words in the dictionary."

Jessie even made a practice science quiz for Casey to complete.

During basketball practice, Casey began to pass the ball to Jessie. At first the other girls were suspicious. Why was Casey being so helpful?

"Don't forget to bend your knees right before you shoot," Casey told Jessie during practice.

Casey's science grade improved, and she stayed on the team. Jessie began to improve in basketball, too.

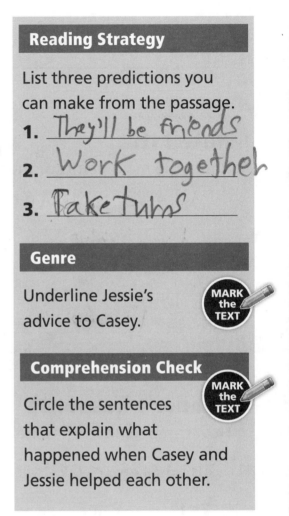

Reading Strategy

List three predictions you can make from the passage.

1. They'll be friends
2. Work together
3. Take turns

Genre

Underline Jessie's advice to Casey.

MARK the TEXT

Comprehension Check

Circle the sentences that explain what happened when Casey and Jessie helped each other.

MARK the TEXT

Use the Strategy

How did previewing and predicting help you understand the passage?

They helped by making you know.

Retell It!

Retell the main points of the passage to a partner.

Casey grades improve and Jessie gets better at basketball. Casey isn't a ball hog anymore and she used to be.

Reader's Response

How can people learn to help each other?

By being nice and helpful, and taking turns.

Retell the passage to a family member.

Name _____ Date _____

Phonics: Short Vowels

Use with Student Book page 16.

~~at~~	~~but~~	~~crop~~	~~fill~~	~~had~~	~~let~~	~~lift~~	~~not~~
~~ox~~	~~pass~~	~~rest~~	~~shut~~	~~then~~	~~trip~~	~~up~~	

A. Sort the words according to their short vowel sounds. One example has been done for you.

Short Vowels				
a	e	i	o	u
pass	let	fill	ox	but
at	then	trip	Not	up
Had	rest	lift	Chop	Shut

B. Sort the words again. This time sort them according to their spelling patterns. One example has been done for you.

Spelling Patterns			
VC	CVC	CVCC	CCVC
at	but	pass	Then
ox	had	lift	Shut
up	let	crop	trip
	not	fill	rest

 Add one more word to each column of both charts. Show your work to a family member.

7

Comprehension: Preview and Predict

Use with Student Book pages 18–19.

**Read the title and the first and last paragraphs of the passage.
Answer the first question. Then read the entire passage and answer the
second question.**

A Good Solution

Tomorrow was Aimee's big tennis match. Everyone was sure Aimee
would win. She was the school's best player.

"What's the matter, Aimee?" asked her coach. "You seem a little
clumsy today. Did you hurt yourself?"

"Coach," she said, "I think it's my arm again."

The coach frowned. He knew Aimee had a sore arm. "Maybe Wanda
should play tomorrow instead of you," he said.

"Wanda hasn't played all week," said Aimee. "She's at her
grandmother's house."

"I have a plan," said the coach. "You go home and put ice on your
arm. I'll call Wanda's grandmother."

1. What do you think the passage will be about?

She will win the tennis match
but get hurt

2. Was your prediction correct? What does the passage tell you that you
could not predict?

I got half right because she does
get hurt but it doesn't say
she won.

Preview a story by reading only the title and the first and last paragraphs.
Share your predictions with a family member. Then read the entire story
together to see if your prediction was correct.

Name _____ Date _____

Grammar: Singular and Plural Nouns

Use with Student Book page 20.

> A **singular noun** is a word that names one person, place, or thing. A **plural noun** is a word that names more than one person, place, or thing.

A. Read each sentence. Underline the singular nouns. Circle the plural nouns.

1. Both ponies won a race.

2. Try not to hit the ball into the bushes!

3. The batter missed the easiest pitches.

4. Put the boxes on the chair.

5. Each team played two games.

B. Write the plural of each noun.

6. class ___classes___

7. winner ___winnerss___

8. berry ___berries___

9. gas ___gases___

10. house ___houses___

 **Home-School Connection** Write five more singular nouns. Then write the plural form of each one. Show your work to a family member.

Spelling: Using a Dictionary

Use with Student Book page 21.

**Read this definition for the word *conduct*.
Use the definition to answer the questions.**

> **con•duct¹** /kən'dʌkt/ *v.* **1.** to control or
> manage **2.** to guide or lead **3.** *MUSIC* to lead
> (a musical group) **4.** to act in a certain way
> **con•duct²** /'kɑndʌkt/ *n.* **1.** the way a person
> or people act **2.** the act of controlling or
> managing

SPELLING TIP

If you are not sure of the spelling of a word, use a dictionary to check the spelling.

1. What parts of speech are shown in the definition for the
word ***conduct***?

_2. Verob, Noun or_____

2. What does the information between the slashes tell you?

_How to pro-nounce_____

3. How many definitions are given for ***conduct*** when it is used as
a noun?

_Type_____

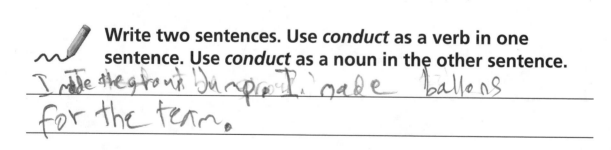

Write two sentences. Use *conduct* as a verb in one
sentence. Use *conduct* as a noun in the other sentence.

I rade the ground bumprou I made ballons

for the tern.

_____

Home-School Connection **Read the dictionary definitions of three words. Tell a family member what
you learned.**

Name _____ Date _____

Vocabulary

Use with Student Book pages 22–23.

A. Choose the word that *best* completes each sentence. Write the word.

1. Doctors who work in unsafe places are

_____ .

2. Many _____ left the country during the war.

3. She had medical _____ so she could help the refugees.

4. Cooperation and _____ helped the people rebuild their village.

5. Aid workers _____ to help people in trouble.

6. People call 911 in an _____ .

Key Words
emergency
courageous
teamwork
training
intervene
refugees

B. Choose the word that *best* matches the meaning of the underlined words. Write the word.

7. With the right <u>instruction</u>, anyone can give first-aid treatment.

_____

8. The doctors will <u>come in and help</u> when disasters strike.

_____

9. Many <u>people who left their countries</u> came to the United States.

_____

11

C. Answer the questions.

10. What do you think a **courageous** person is like?

_____

11. What is one type of **emergency**?

_____

12. Why might a teacher **intervene** on the playground?

_____

13. What is an example of **teamwork**?

_____

14. What is one job where you might need **training**?

_____

15. Why might people become **refugees**?

_____

Academic Words

D. Read each sentence. Write a new sentence using the underlined word.

16. The teacher had to <u>evaluate</u> the results of the test.

_____

17. The volunteers' first <u>task</u> was to take care of the people who were hurt.

_____

 Write a sentence for each key word. Share your sentences with a family member.

Name _____ Date _____

Reader's Companion

Use with Student Book pages 24–29.

Doctors Without Borders

In 2004, there was a tsunami, or tidal wave, in South Asia. The tsunami destroyed many towns. Many people were hurt or killed.

Doctors Without Borders worked for more than a year in countries that were hit by the tsunami. They gave people shots to make sure they did not get sick. The doctors gave people supplies like tents and clothing. They talked to people about what had happened. Sometimes just being there to listen to the victims helped the most.

Sometimes the volunteers help people in a town build new hospitals. That involves real teamwork!

Sometimes the best help the volunteers can give is training. It can be better for Doctors Without Borders to help train local doctors to take care of people after a crisis. The local doctors can give care to sick and hurt people after Doctors Without Borders leaves the area.

Use What You Know

List three things you already know about doctors.

1. _____

2. _____

3. _____

Genre

Underline two things Doctors Without Borders did after the tsunami.

MARK the TEXT

Comprehension Check

Circle the part of the text that explains why training is important for Doctors Without Borders.

MARK the TEXT

Use the Strategy

How did using your prior knowledge help you understand the passage?

_____

_____

_____

Summarize It!

Summarize the passage for a partner.

_____

_____

_____

_____

Reader's Response

Would you like to volunteer for Doctors without Borders? Why or why not?

_____

_____

_____

Summarize the passage for a family member.

Name _____ Date _____

Phonics: Long Vowels with Silent e

Use with Student Book page 30.

Silent e Rule
When the first vowel (V) in a one-syllable word is followed by a consonant (C) and an e, the vowel is usually long. The final e is silent.

A. Underline the words in the box that follow the CVCe pattern. Circle the words that are exceptions to the silent e rule.

bare	bride	cave	cone	dime	dove
glove	move	mule	one	pole	rake
some	state	theme	tune	were	

B. Choose five words. Write a sentence for each word.

_____

_____

_____

_____

_____

 Write five more words with the CVCe pattern. Share your words with a family member.

Comprehension: Activate Prior Knowledge

Use with Student Book pages 32–33.

Read the passage. Answer the questions.

What Do Nurses Do?

Nurses work hard to keep people healthy. They keep an eye on patients' temperatures, blood pressures, and vital signs. Nurses work in many different places. Some nurses work in doctors' offices. Other nurses work in hospitals. Some of them even work in the operating room!

Nurses work with both patients and doctors to make sure patients get the best care. They teach patients about their conditions and how to take care of themselves. They tell the doctors if the patient is having trouble with medication or medical equipment. They call the doctor right away if the patient has a life-threatening condition. They are often the first people an accident victim sees in the emergency room.

1. Describe something you know about nurses.

_____

_____

_____

2. Describe how nurses help patients or doctors.

_____

_____

_____

 **Share what you have learned about Doctors Without Borders with a family member.**

Name _____ Date _____

Grammar: Past Tense Verbs

Use with Student Book page 34.

Write the past tense form of each verb. Use each verb in a sentence.

1. try _____

_____

2. flip _____

_____

3. help _____

_____

4. care _____

_____

5. hurry _____

_____

6. pull _____

_____

7. grab _____

_____

8. cry _____

_____

Home-School Connection Write the past tense forms of three more verbs. Show your work to a family member.

17

Spelling: Plural Nouns

Use with Student Book page 35.

Use the correct form of the noun to complete each sentence.

1. We bought the children some new _____ .
   (toy/toys)

2. I went to the library to get some _____
   (book/books)

3. Wooden _____ are hard to sit on. (bench/benches)

4. Dad ate both _____ of ice cream. (bowl/bowls)

5. I work for a _____ that makes cars.
   (company/companies)

6. The price of _____ is high. (gas/gases)

7. All the _____ in town sell fresh bread. (bakery/
   bakeries)

 Choose two of the word pairs in parentheses. Write a paragraph using both the singular and plural forms of the words.

_____

_____

_____

_____

 **Write the plural form of three objects you see around you. Show your work to a family member.**

Name _____ Date _____

Vocabulary

Use with Student Book pages 36–37.

Copyright © by Pearson Education, Inc.

A. Choose the word that *best* completes each sentence. Write the word.

1. Will you help me _____ this stack of books?

2. There was enough food to

_____ with everyone.

3. I _____ inside to see what was there.

4. The one-room _____ had a straw roof.

5. Water was _____ because it had not rained in months.

6. Watch the elephants _____ the lions.

B. Choose the word that *best* matches the meaning of the underlined words. Write the word.

7. She <u>took a secret look</u> while no one was around.

_____

8. The roof of our <u>small house</u> leaks when it rains. _____

9. They burned dried grass because wood was <u>hard to find</u>.

_____

10. Watch them <u>run quickly</u> into the pool! _____

11. Will you <u>give me part of</u> your sandwich? _____

Key Words
carry
scarce
share
peeked
cottage
charge

C. Answer the questions.

12. How can you save water when it is **scarce**?

_____

13. What did you **carry** to school today?

_____

14. Why is it a bad idea to **charge** toward something?

_____

15. How would you describe a **cottage**?

_____

16. When have you **peeked** at something?

_____

17. Why do brothers and sisters **share**?

_____

Academic Words

D. Read each sentence. Write a new sentence using the underlined word.

18. Math class is easier when I have a good <u>attitude</u>.

_____

19. The teacher asked me to put one <u>item</u> in the box.

_____

 Home-School Connection Write a sentence for each key word. Share your sentences with a family member.

Name _____ Date _____

Reader's Companion

Use with Student Book pages 38–43.

Stone Soup

One of John's favorite things was a big iron pot. The pot had once belonged to his mother.

As much as he loved the pot, John was hungry. He decided to trade the pot for something to eat.

"I'm sorry," said the farmer's wife from her cottage door. "Food is scarce these days. I only have enough for my own family."

"Thank you, anyway," John said. "I will carry my pot to the next village."

John walked many miles.

"May I trade this nice iron pot for something to eat?" he asked everyone he saw.

But the people in this village were just as poor and hungry as John was.

As John started to leave the village, he saw a smooth, round stone in the road. If only this stone were something good to eat, he thought.

Then John got an idea. He filled his iron pot with water. He gathered sticks and dry wood and then built a blazing fire all around his pot.

Reading Strategy

List three events in this passsage.

1. _____

2. _____

3. _____

Genre

MARK the TEXT

A folktale is often a very old story. Underline a sentence that gives a clue that this is an old story.

Comprehension Check

MARK the TEXT

Circle the text that tells why John wanted to trade his pot.

Use the Strategy

How did identifying events in the plot help you understand
the story?

_____

_____

_____

Retell It!

Retell the passage as if you are the main character.

_____

_____

_____

_____

Reader's Response

What did you learn about helping others in this story?

_____

_____

_____

Copyright © by Pearson Education, Inc.

 **Retell the passage to a family member.**

Name _____ Date _____

Word Analysis: Multiple-Meaning Words

Use with Student Book page 44.

Read each sentence. Put a check by the best meaning for the word in boldface type.

1. The sand felt hot and **dry**.

_____ **a.** not wet, such as *a dry riverbed*
_____ **b.** without enough oil, such as *dry skin*

2. The rising waters overran the **bank** of the canal.

_____ **a.** business that holds people's money, such as *a savings bank*
_____ **b.** steep side of a body of water, such as *a riverbank*

3. What was the first **state** in our country?

_____ **a.** to say out loud or in writing, such as *state your name*
_____ **b.** an area of land that is part of a larger country, such as *the state of New York*

4. Jason can **run** fast.

_____ **a.** to try to be elected to an office
_____ **b.** to move very quickly

5. John went to the **spring** to get water.

_____ **a.** a place where water comes up from the ground
_____ **b.** a coiled piece of metal

Think of a word that has at least two different meanings. Write a sentence for each meaning. Share your sentences with a family member.

23

Comprehension: Events in a Plot

Use with Student Book pages 46–47.

Read the passage. Then write E for Event and D for Detail.

Stone Soup

John picked up his pot and headed home. Shortly after he started walking down the dirt road, he came across a perfectly round stone. "I wish this stone were something good to eat," he thought.

Then John got an idea.

He went back to the village, gathered up some wood, and began to build a fire. He dropped the stone into the pot.

Soon, a girl in a red dress came by with some potatoes. Then a boy came over and dropped some bright, orange carrots into the soup. As the vegetables began to cook, more people from the village noticed the smells. They started to bring more vegetables, meat, and spices.

John saw how hungry the villagers looked. "Will you stay and share this soup with me?" he asked.

1. _____ The stone was perfectly round.

2. _____ John dropped the stone in the pot.

3. _____ John gathered some wood and built a fire.

4. _____ The girl was wearing a red dress.

5. _____ The carrots were bright orange.

6. _____ People from the village brought vegetables, meat, and spices.

Home-School Connection Have a family member read or tell you a story. (The family member can use his or her own language.) Talk about the events and details in the story.

24

Name _____ Date _____

Grammar: Future Tense Verbs

Use with Student Book page 48.

A. Put a check by each sentence that tells about something that will happen in the future.

_____ **1.** I ate lunch after my friend came over.

_____ **2.** Everyone will be at the play!

_____ **3.** Did you talk on the phone yesterday?

_____ **4.** We will study together on Saturday.

_____ **5.** We will have lunch together tomorrow.

_____ **6.** The party was wonderful!

B. Write the future-tense form of each verb. Use the helping verb *will*.

7. decide _____

8. visit _____

9. exclaim _____

10. try _____

11. go _____

12. study _____

Write three sentences about something you will do in the future. Share your sentences with a family member.

25

Spelling: Compound Words

Use with Student Book page 49.

S P E L L I N G
T I P

When trying to spell compound words, look for a smaller word within the larger word.

A. Use the two words to write a new word. The first one is done for you.

1. door   knob   <u>doorknob</u>

2. grand   mother   _____

3. under   ground   _____

4. house   boat   _____

5. sand   paper   _____

B. Use each word to help you form a compound word. Some examples have more than one choice.

6. day   <u>daytime or Sunday</u>

7. light   _____

8. water   _____

9. seat   _____

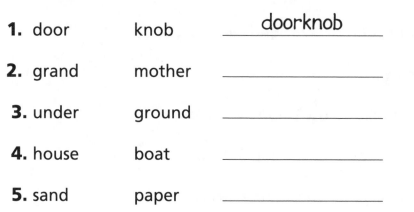

Choose four of the words you wrote. Use each word in a sentence.

_____

_____

_____

_____

 Home-School Connection   Write three more compound words. Circle the words that make up the compound words. Share your work with a family member.

Name _____ Date _____

Review

Use with Student Book pages 2–49.

Answer the questions after reading Unit 1. You can go back and reread to help find the answers.

1. In *Everybody Wins*, imagine that Jessie did not help Casey with her science homework. How would the story be different? Write your prediction.

_____

_____

_____

2. Which sentence does NOT use the word *improve* correctly? Circle the letter of the correct answer.

    a. Studying for the test helped you improve your grade.

    b. Practice will help you improve your basketball game.

    c. Not paying attention in class will improve my grades.

    d. Jessie practiced hard to improve her basketball skills.

3. How did your prior knowledge about doctors help you understand *Doctors Without Borders*?

_____

_____

_____

4. Which word has the same meaning as *courageous*? Circle the letter of the correct answer.

    a. weak   **c.** afraid

    b. brave   **d.** strong

5. Refer to the KWL Chart you completed on page 33 in the Student Book. Complete the sentences.

    a. I already know _____ about Doctors Without Borders.

    b. I want to learn _____ about Doctors Without Borders.

    c. I learned _____ about Doctors Without Borders.

6. In *Stone Soup,* what did John do when he found the stone in the road? Circle the letter of the correct answer.

    a. He threw the stone into the river.

    b. He got an idea to make stone soup.

    c. He tried to trade the stone for food.

    d. He put the stone in his pocket.

7. Name some of the items John and the villagers put in the soup.

_____

_____

8. What lesson did John teach the girl when he gave the stone to her?

_____

_____

_____

_____

Copyright © by Pearson Education, Inc.

Tell a family member something new you learned in this unit.

Name _____ Date _____

Vocabulary

Use with Student Book pages 62–63.

Copyright © by Pearson Education, Inc.

Key Words

cooperate
bore
marvelous
millet
virtue
grateful

A. Choose the word that _best_ completes each sentence. Write the word.

1. John was _____ for his home, his family, and his friends.

2. Kofi and Jelani left sacks of

   _____ for the horses.

3. George's mother said honesty is a _____ .

4. When we _____ , we finish our work quickly.

5. The trees _____ a lot of fruit.

6. We had a _____ time at the party!

B. Underline the key word in the row of letters. Then write a sentence for each word.

7. vreohgmarvelousnvrhg _____

8. ewruhfbhwmilletuwebhc _____

9. ewgvcooperatevbiur _____

10. fuebevgratefulruvb _____

11. ughouviuvbvirtuevnrenv _____

12. gugnvabborervnvbvm _____

C. Answer the questions.

13. When do you feel **grateful**?

_____

14. What can **millet** be used to make?

_____

15. Why do you think kindness is a **virtue**?

_____

16. When is it good to **cooperate**?

_____

17. What types of trees **bore** fruit?

_____

18. When might you have a **marvelous** time?

_____

Academic Words

D. Read each sentence. Write a new sentence using the underlined word.

19. The villagers had to <u>assess</u> the damage from the mudslide.

_____

20. The cake tasted funny because Mom made an <u>error</u> in following the recipe.

_____

 Use each key word in a sentence. Share your sentences with a family member.

Name _____ Date _____

Reader's Companion

Use with Student Book pages 64–69.

The Three Gifts

When Ada finished school, she went to other villages where she worked hard to help people. Ada's brothers and sisters admired her. She sent drawings of the school she helped to build. Ada wrote that it was a big job, but lots of fun.

One by one, Ada's brothers and sisters finished school. They all asked Jelani if they could go and help people. Jelani's eyes filled with joy each time, and he said, "Yes, you can help people."

In time, only the youngest son remained at home. His name was Kofi. Kofi loved to receive his siblings' letters. One brother helped dig wells for fresh water. Another brother helped farmers plant better crops. A sister helped a village hold an election to choose a better leader.

All of the letters were alike in one way. They all invited Kofi and Jelani to visit their villages.

Use What You Know

List three things a hero needs.

1. _____

2. _____

3. _____

Genre

MARK the TEXT

Who is a hero in this passage? Underline where you found your answer.

Reading Strategy

MARK the TEXT

Circle the parts of the passage that help you understand the plot.

Use the Strategy

How did identifying the characters and plot help you understand
the story?

_____

_____

_____

Retell It!

Retell the passage from Kofi's point of view.

_____

_____

_____

_____

Reader's Response

Why do you think Ada and her brothers and sisters like to help others?

_____

_____

_____

Retell the passage to a family member.

Name _____ Date _____

Phonics: Long Vowel Pairs

Use with Student Book page 70.

> **Long vowel pairs** can be spelled in different ways. Some long vowel pairs are spelled with two vowels. Read each word. The first vowel is long. The second vowel is silent.

Long Vowel Pairs				
Long *a*	**Long e**	**Long *i***	**Long o**	**Long *u***
h<u>ay</u>	m<u>ea</u>t	p<u>ie</u>	f<u>oe</u>	s<u>ui</u>t
r<u>ai</u>n	f<u>ee</u>t		<u>oa</u>k	d<u>ue</u>

Find two words in each sentence that have long vowel pairs. Write the words. Circle the letters that make the long vowel pairs.

1. Did you eat a piece of fruit today?

_____   _____

2. We used to live on a main road.

_____   _____

3. He paid for the seeds with a $20 bill.

_____   _____

 **Write another word for each of the vowel pairs above. Share your work with a family member.**

Comprehension: Characters and Plot

Use with Student Book pages 72–73.

Read the passage. Answer the questions.

The Deal

Fall had arrived, and the corn was ready to be picked. Farmer Joe didn't know what to do. He had just broken his leg. "How am I going to harvest my crop?" he thought. Farmer Joe stood on his front porch and shook his head. "Hey there," said Jamal. "I'm your new neighbor." Farmer Joe waved. "Looks like your corn is ready," Jamal continued. Farmer Joe smiled and pointed to the cast on his leg. Jamal looked at the leg. Then he looked out at the cornfield and said, "I'll make a deal. I'll pick your corn, if you help me paint my house next spring." Farmer Joe was happy. He said, "You've got yourself a deal!"

1. Who are the characters? _____

2. Underline the main events in the passage.

3. What is the plot of the passage?

_____

_____

_____

Summarize the plot of this passage in your own words. Share your work with a family member.

Name _____   Date _____

Grammar: Adjectives and Adverbs

Use with Student Book page 74.

> **Adjectives** describe nouns. An adjective can come before or after the noun it describes.

Read the sentences. Underline the adjectives. Then draw a box around the adverbs.

1. The wild horse angrily kicked the barn door.

2. Suddenly, a warm rain began to fall.

3. The wooden cart creaked noisily.

4. I know exactly where you left your work clothes.

5. My little brother carefully read each word.

6. They worked steadily in the hot sun.

7. The boys ate their large lunch quickly.

8. Martina took me quickly to see the adorable pandas.

9. The red train moved slowly.

10. The tall waiter skillfully carried his tray.

Write five nouns. Then write five adjectives to go with them. Do the same for verbs and adverbs. Share your work with a family member.

35

Spelling: *ch* and *sh* Sounds

Use with Student Book page 75.

A. Read each word. Pay attention to the sounds.

ar<u>ch</u>es	<u>ch</u>ip	ou<u>ch</u>
fi<u>sh</u>	<u>sh</u>ip	wi<u>sh</u>es

SPELLING TIP

When the letters *c* and *h* or *s* and *h* are together in a word, they make one sound.

Choose four words. Write a sentence for each word.

1. _____

2. _____

3. _____

4. _____

B. Circle the words with the letters *ch* or *sh*. Write each word on the line. Then underline the consonant digraphs.

5. Which show do you like the best? _____

6. Our child likes to go fishing. _____

 Write a journal entry using at least five words that have the digraphs *ch* or *sh*.

_____

_____

_____

 Write six more words that have the digraphs *ch* or *sh*. Write a definition of each word in your own words. Share your work with a family member.

Name _____ Date _____

Vocabulary

Use with Student Book pages 76–77.

Key Words

chased
arena
swollen
wander
criminal

A. Choose the word that *best* completes each sentence. Write the word.

1. Many exciting events took place

in the _____ .

2. The lion _____ its next meal into the woods.

3. Only a _____ would rob a bank.

4. I knew my arm was broken because it was really

_____ .

5. We saw a lost puppy _____ through the neighborhood.

B. Write TRUE or FALSE.

6. Sports teams sometimes play in an arena. _____

7. A criminal would never break the law. _____

8. People wander when they are not in a hurry. _____

9. Cats chase mice. _____

10. Swollen body parts never hurt. _____

C. Answer the questions.

11. When have you **chased** a person or animal?

_____

12. Have you ever seen a **swollen** body part? Describe it.

_____

13. What makes a person a **criminal**?

_____

14. What kinds of sports do you play in an **arena**?

_____

15. Where would you like to **wander**?

_____

Academic Words

D. Read each sentence. Write a new sentence using the underlined word.

16. Androcles's <u>motive</u> was to help the lion.

_____

17. The lion believed in the <u>principle</u> of helping others.

_____

Use each key word in a sentence. Share your sentences with a family member.

Name _____ Date _____

Reader's Companion

Use with Student Book pages 78–79.

Brave Androcles

Not just any ordinary lion, his friend.
The lion was as sweet as sugar.
He was as quiet as a mouse.
All he did was wander around the arena.
He did not . . .

      bite.

      eat.

      growl.

next?
Master was . . .

      shocked.

      amazed.

      confused.

And Androcles was a hero.
Never bothered again,
          WHEW!

Use What You Know

List ways helping others can make you a hero.

1. _____

2. _____

3. _____

Genre: Poetry

MARK the TEXT

Underline the word patterns you see in this passage.

Reading Strategy

MARK the TEXT

Circle words that describe when you may have felt like Androcles.

Use the Strategy

Why is it helpful to make connections when you read?

_____

_____

_____

Retell It!

Retell what happens in the passage from the lion's point of view.

_____

_____

_____

_____

Reader's Response

Has anything unexpected ever happened to you? Was it shocking?
Amazing? Confusing? Write about the experience.

_____

_____

_____

Home-School Connection   Retell the passage to a family member.

Name _____ Date _____

Phonics: Vowel Pair *ea*

Use with Student Book page 80.

> The vowel pair *ea* can have the long *e* sound,
> as in *eat*, or the short *e* sound, as in *head*.

A. Read each word. Write whether the vowel pair *ea* has the long *e* sound or the short *e* sound.

1. team _____

2. head _____

3. lean _____

4. thread _____

5. steam _____

6. bread _____

B. Read each sentence. Find the word with the *ea* vowel pair. Circle the word if it has the long *e* sound. Draw a box around the word if it has the short *e* sound.

7. I ran so fast I couldn't catch my breath.

8. Having steak for dinner is a treat!

9. She used blue thread to sew her dress.

10. Each kid had a beach ball.

 **Home-School Connection** Write sentences for five words that have the *ea* vowel pair. Share your sentences with a family member.

41

Comprehension: Make Connections

Use with Student Book pages 82–83.

A. Read the passage. Answer the questions as they relate to your life.

The Class Project

Helen noticed how ugly the benches looked. Most of the paint had chipped or peeled away. Justine sat down as Helen looked at the bench across the path. That bench needed to be painted, too.

"Hi," said Justine.

Helen turned her head quickly. "I think I have an idea for the class project," she said. Last year, they planted trees on Main Street.

"What's your idea?" asked Justine.

"I think we should repaint all these park benches," Helen said. "I'll bet it has been years since they were last painted."

Justine nodded. "I think we've got ourselves a project!" she said. "Remember last year? We had the best time!"

1. What special place do you like to visit?

_____

_____

_____

2. What would you like to do to help your community?

_____

_____

_____

 Share your answers to the questions with a family member.

Name _____   Date _____

Grammar: Pronouns

Use with Student Book page 84.

Subject Pronouns	I, you, he, she, it, we, they
Object Pronouns	me, you, him, her, it, us, them

Read each sentence. Circle the pronoun. Then write if it is a subject or an object pronoun.

1. Why was she going to the park? _____

2. This big box is for her. _____

3. Malcolm and I never have anything to do.

   _____

4. All of the animals belonged to them. _____

5. Will you give Frank this letter? _____

6. We worked until the sun set. _____

7. Loretta is going to bake a cake for you. _____

8. Look at us! _____

9. They went to the store. _____

10. Give it to her. _____

 **Write five sentences using different pronouns. Share your sentences with a family member.**

Spelling: /k/ Sound Spelled with the Letter c

Use with Student Book page 85.

A. Read the words. Circle the words that begin with the /k/ sound spelled c.

1. class
2. cool
3. chase

4. chew
5. car
6. connect

SPELLING TIP

When the letter *c* is followed by *a, o,* or *u,* as in *cat, cone,* or *cub,* it stands for the sound /k/.

car	cat	cone	cub	cut

B. Read each clue. Write the word that matches the clue.

7. something you put ice cream in _____

8. your mom or dad drives this _____

9. you can do this with scissors _____

 Write a journal entry using at least four words with the /k/ sound spelled *c.*

_____

_____

_____

_____

 Think of five more words that have the /k/ sound spelled *c.* Write a sentence for each word. Share your work with a family member.

Name _____ Date _____

Vocabulary

Use with Student Book pages 86–87.

Key Words

blister
contained
broad
midst
merry
startle

A. Choose the word that *best* completes each sentence. Write the word.

1. Emily sat in the _____ of her lifelong friends.

2. My suitcase _____ clothes and shoes.

3. The street was as _____ as a wide highway.

4. Why did you _____ me with that loud noise?

5. That will _____ in the hot sun!

6. The old man had _____ eyes that smiled.

B. Write the word that *best* matches the definition.

7. to frighten suddenly _____

8. to bubble and peel _____

9. to be happy and joyful _____

10. a state of being wide _____

11. in the middle _____

12. to be in something _____

C. Answer the questions.

13. What objects may have **contained** other objects?

_____

14. When might you sit in the **midst** of something?

_____

15. What things might **blister**?

_____

16. When might you be **merry**?

_____

17. What kinds of things **startle** you?

_____

18. What might a **broad** street look like?

_____

Academic Words

D. Read each sentence. Write a new sentence using the underlined word.

19. Dorothy had to <u>interact</u> with the Munchkins.

_____

20. Dorothy's dress had <u>distinct</u> features.

_____

Use each key word in a sentence. Share your sentences with a family member.

Name _____ Date _____

Reader's Companion

Use with Student Book pages 88–93.

The Wizard of Oz

Dorothy was startled when she woke up. The house had landed gently on the ground. Bright sunshine poured through the windows' unbroken panes.

A beautiful new world appeared. There were huge flowers, tall trees, and a small, sparkling brook.

It was nothing like the farm in Kansas.

A group of people walked toward Dorothy. They were all very small. Their clothes contained every color of the rainbow. Dorothy thought they were children. Then she saw that some of the people had long beards. Some of the people had white hair and wrinkled faces.

"Welcome to Oz, brave witch," a woman said. "We are so grateful to you for killing the Wicked Witch of the East. Now the Munchkins are free!"

Use What You Know

List three things Dorothy saw when she woke up in Oz.

1. _____

2. _____

3. _____

Genre: Fantasy

MARK the TEXT

Circle the words in the passage that help you understand that the passage is a fantasy.

Comprehension Check

MARK the TEXT

How did Dorothy know she was no longer in Kansas? Underline the text where you found your answer.

Use the Strategy

How did identifying the problems and solutions help you understand the passage?

_____

_____

_____

Retell It!

Retell this passage as if you are the main character.

_____

_____

_____

_____

Reader's Response

What would you do if you found yourself in a strange place?

_____

_____

_____

Home-School Connection   **Retell the passage to a family member.**

Name _____ Date _____

Word Analysis: Word Origins

Use with Student Book page 94.

> **Some of the words you use every day come from other languages.**

| canoe | chocolate | queen | tennis |

Read the words. Then read about the words. Match each word with its description.

1. The name of this female ruler comes from the German word *qino* and later the English word *cwene* which meant "woman."

_____

2. This word names a dessert or flavoring. It comes from *tchocoatl*, a word in Nahuatl, the language of the Aztecs. This group lived in Mexico.

_____

3. This word names a type of wooden dugout boat. The word is taken from *canaoua*, a word from the Arawak, a Native American group on the island of Haiti. Columbus introduced the word to Spain where it became the Spanish *canoa*.

_____

4. The name of this sport comes from the French word *tenez*, a form of the verb *tenir*. The meaning of *tenir* is "there you go." Players would say "tenez" when they hit the ball during a game.

_____

Think of five words that come from another language. (You may use your own language.) Look up the words in the dictionary to learn about their origins. Ask a family member to help you.

Comprehension: Characters and Conflicts

Use with Student Book pages 96–97.

Read the passage. Then answer the questions.

The Chiprock

The planet had become very cold. There was ice and snow everywhere. The Chiprock found it hard to grow their crops. They could not hunt for food because the animals could not run on the ice. The Chiprock could not even walk on it. Gunk, their leader, decided it was best to move underground.

Many of the Chiprock were unhappy about moving underground. After all, they had some luck growing crops indoors. Gunk's son and his friends were teaching the others to skate on the ice.

Gunk called a meeting of the tribe's leaders to discuss the issue. After many hours of debating and voting, they decided to stay above ground.

1. What are the conflicts in this passage?

_____

_____

2. Is Gunk's main conflict with himself or with the Chiprock? Why?

_____

_____

3. What do you know about Gunk's character?

_____

_____

Write at least three sentences about a character and a conflict. Share your sentences with a family member.

Name _____ Date _____

Grammar: Possessive Nouns

Use with Student Book page 98.

To make a singular noun possessive, add an apostrophe (') and *s*.	To make a plural noun that ends in -*s* possessive, add an apostrophe (').	To make a plural noun that does not end in -*s* possessive, add an apostrophe (') and *s*.

Read each phrase. Write S if the underlined noun is singular or P if it is plural. Then rewrite the phrase making the noun possessive.

1. the bed belonging to the <u>dog</u>

_____ _____

2. the cakes made by the <u>bakers</u>

_____ _____

3. the heat of the <u>sun</u>

_____ _____

4. the cars belonging to the <u>women</u>

_____ _____

5. the bikes belonging to the <u>kids</u>

_____ _____

6. the smell of the <u>flower</u>

_____ _____

 **Write five nouns in their possessive forms. Share your work with a family member.**

Spelling: Words with Apostrophes

Use with Student Book page 99.

do not can also be written as **don't**
I <u>do not</u> want that. / I <u>don't</u> want that. * The apostrophe takes the place of the letter *o* in *not*.

Follow the model above. Leave out a letter and add an apostrophe to write another form of the words.

1. should not _____

2. it will _____

3. he is _____

4. are not _____

5. they are _____

6. can not _____

 Write a short paragraph using words with contractions.

_____

_____

_____

_____

 Write a paragraph that includes some of the contractions you studied. Circle the contractions. Then write the complete words. Share your work with a family member.

Name _____ Date _____

Review

Use with Student Book pages 56–99.

Answer the questions after reading Unit 2. You can go back and reread to help find the answers.

1. Which character do you think is the hero in *The Three Gifts*? Why?

_____

_____

_____

2. What are the three gifts in the story?

_____

_____

_____

3. Underline the words that show cause and effect in the passage.

Jelani called out, "Stop everyone!" Jelani's advisors were soon teaching the others how to build a wood house. The people said, "You have helped us with this house. Now we can use these skills to build a whole village. One day, you will call on us, and we will return the favor."

4. Make a connection to how you feel about Androcles after reading *Brave Androcles*. Describe a time when you have felt scared.

_____

_____

_____

5. Read this line from the poem.

> Something had to be done.

What had to be done?

_____

_____

_____

6. In the *Wizard of Oz,* why did Dorothy stay in the house when the tornado came? Circle the letter of the correct answer.

   a. She wanted to watch the house spin around.
   b. She thought the tornado was interesting.
   c. She wanted to rescue Toto from under the bed.
   d. She was angry with Aunt Em and Uncle Henry.

7. Do you think Dorothy's journey as a hero is beginning or ending in this reading? Why?

_____

_____

8. Why is Dorothy a hero in this story?

_____

_____

Home-School Connection   Tell a family member something new you learned from this unit.

Name _____ Date _____

Vocabulary

Use with Student Book pages 112–113.

Copyright © by Pearson Education, Inc.

A. Choose the word that *best* completes each sentence. Write the word.

Key Words
colonies
crown
adversary
taxes
liberty
representation

1. People coming to New York City are greeted by

the Statue of _____ .

2. Some of the earliest British _____

were Massachusetts, Virginia, and Pennsylvania.

3. The colonists did not want to be controlled by the British

_____ .

4. The British government forced people to pay

_____ on many things.

5. Some people felt King George was a friend, while others felt he was

an _____ .

6. The colonists cried, "No taxation without _____ !"

B. Read each sentence. Write TRUE or FALSE.

7. The government makes people pay taxes. _____

8. Guam was one of the early British colonies in North America.

_____

9. The British crown was the king and his government. _____

C. Answer the questions.

10. When do people pay **taxes**?

_____

11. Why is **representation** important in government?

_____

12. How does **crown** describe the British government?

_____

13. When might you have an **adversary**?

_____

14. Why do you think **liberty** is important to people?

_____

15. What were some of the first **colonies** in North America?

_____

Academic Words

D. Read each sentence. Write a new sentence using the underlined word.

16. I made a <u>contract</u> with my teacher to learn ten new words each day.

_____

17. Johnnie agreed to <u>compensate</u> my dad for the broken window.

_____

 **Home-School Connection** Use each Key Word in a sentence. Share your sentences with a family member.

Name _____ Date _____

Reader's Companion

Use with Student Book pages 114–119.

Writing a Great Speech

A speech should have a beginning, a middle, and an end. Make sure each part helps the audience follow your ideas.

The beginning is important. A good beginning gives the speech's theme. The beginning of the speech should also fit the theme. A joke at the start of a speech may not go with a serious theme. A good beginning makes people interested in what you have to say. It will stay in a listener's mind.

The middle of the speech explains your theme. It gives reasons and facts. It should have a true story or a real-life example of your theme.

The ending tells your theme again in a new way. In a few words, connect the theme to your facts. Keep your purpose in mind. End your speech by asking the audience to take action or agree with your ideas.

Use What You Know

List three things a good speech needs.

1. _____

2. _____

3. _____

Comprehension Check

MARK the TEXT

Where is the best place to introduce the theme of a speech? Circle the text where you found the answer.

Reading Strategy

MARK the TEXT

Underline the part of the passage that describes the middle of the speech.

Use the Strategy

How did comparing and contrasting help you understand the passage?

_____

_____

_____

Summarize It!

Summarize the main points of the passage in your own words.

_____

_____

_____

_____

Reader's Response

What topic would you like to give a speech about? Why?

_____

_____

_____

Copyright © by Pearson Education, Inc.

Home-School Connection   **Summarize the main points of the passage for a family member.**

Name _____ Date _____

Phonics: *R*-controlled *ar, or, ore*

Use with Student Book page 120.

> The letters **ar** usually have the vowel sound found in *arm*. The letters *or* and *ore* usually have the vowel sounds found in *torn* and *tore*.

Read each row of words. Circle the two words that have the same vowel sound.

1.	bark	door	art
2.	important	crown	corner
3.	march	arm	more
4.	orange	orbit	harm
5.	horn	hard	horse
6.	chart	party	more
7.	farm	work	garden
8.	store	share	shore
9.	purpose	porch	story
10.	rather	farther	charm

Write a poem using rhyming word pairs with the /ar/ sound in *arm* or the /or/, /ore/ sounds in *torn* and *tore*. Share your poem with a family member.

Comprehension: Compare and Contrast

Use with Student Book pages 122–123.

Read the passage. Pay attention to things that are similar and different. Then answer the questions.

Training for the Big Race

My friends Maurice and Angelina are getting ready for the big race. They have been training for weeks. Maurice works out every morning for two hours. He likes to train before he goes to school. Angelina also trains for two hours every day. She likes to work out in the afternoon, after school. Angelina spends 30 minutes in the gym. Then she goes running for 45 minutes. Next, she swims for 30 minutes. Maurice also goes to the gym for 30 minutes. He runs for 45 minutes, too. He does not go swimming, though. He rides his bike instead. Both of my friends are working very hard. They can't wait for the big day!

1. How is Maurice's and Angelina's training similar?

_____

_____

2. How is their training different?

_____

_____

 Compare and contrast two objects in your home. Share your work with a family member.

Name _____ Date _____

Grammar: Subject-Verb Agreement

Use with Student Book page 124.

> **When the subject is a singular noun or *he, she,*
> or *it,* add *-s* to the verb.**
>
> The girl *eats* lunch.   She *eats* lunch.
>
> **When the subject is a plural noun or *I, we, you,*
> or *they,* do not add *-s* to the verb.**
>
> His friends **eat.**   They **eat.**

Write the correct form of each verb.

1. start   My friends _____ their homework
after school.

2. look   That apple _____ yummy!

3. play   The team _____ soccer on Mondays.

4. meet   I usually _____ my friends after school.

5. travel   Many people _____ to the beach
in summer.

6. melt   Ice _____ when it's hot.

7. want   Alice _____ to be a doctor.

8. escape   Birds sometimes _____ from
their cages.

**Write sentences for two more verbs, making sure to use proper
subject-verb agreement. Share your sentences with a family member.**

Spelling: Spelling *i* and *e* Together

Use with Student Book page 125.

A. Write the word that *best* fits each clue.

ceiling	fried	friend
neighbor	receiving	tie

SPELLING TIP

When *i* and *e* appear together in a word, *i* is usually before *e*. But watch out, the exceptions can be tricky!

1. the top of a room _____

2. someone you work and play with

_____

3. a person who lives next door _____

4. something you do to your shoelaces _____

5. giving is better than _____

6. some foods are cooked this way _____

Write a paragraph using some of the words in the box.

_____

_____

_____

 Home-School Connection Write five more words that have the letters *i* and *e* together. Explain the Spelling Tip to a family member.

Name _____ Date _____

Vocabulary

Use with Student Book pages 126–127.

Key Words

- delegates
- confidential
- privy
- secrecy
- merchants
- tailors
- cobblestone
- curious

A. Choose the word that *best* completes each sentence. Write the word.

1. Mom made me take a vow of

_____ before she told me

about Jane's surprise party.

2. I am _____ to find out what

is in that box.

3. It is a good idea to keep your personal information

_____ .

4. When we go shopping, we visit many of the

_____ in town.

5. A bathroom was called a _____ in 1787.

6. The horses sometimes found it hard to walk on the

_____ streets.

7. _____ from the new colonies attended the

Constitutional Convention in 1787.

8. _____ work hard to make sure our suits fit well.

B. Answer the questions.

9. Why did the **delegates** keep the meeting **confidential**?

_____

10. Where might you see a **cobblestone** street or path?

_____

11. Where do **merchants** and **tailors** work?

_____

12. When do you get **curious** about something?

_____

13. Where might you find a **privy** today?

_____

14. Why might something be done in **secrecy**?

_____

Academic Words

C. Read each sentence. Write a new sentence using the underlined word.

15. I am an <u>individual</u> in my classroom of students.

_____

16. Ann had to make sure it was <u>legal</u> to have a yard sale.

_____

 **Use each key word in a sentence. Share your sentences with a family member.**

Name _____ Date _____

Reader's Companion

Use with Student Book pages 128–131.

One Hot Summer in Philadelphia

Water sometimes made people sick in the 1780s. People had no way of knowing if their drinking water was clean. To be safe, people didn't drink much plain water. They drank cider, milk, tea, and coffee. They could boil water for tea and coffee.

Houses did not have bathrooms. People used buckets to carry water from nearby wells to their houses. They filled washbowls and pitchers with water to clean their hands and faces. People didn't take baths very often. When they did, they would set a big wooden tub in front of the kitchen fire. After they filled the tub, a whole family would bathe in the same water. The person who went last didn't get very clean!

Like the well, the toilet was outside. It was in a separate building called a privy.

Use What You Know

List three ways life was different in 1787.

1. _____

2. _____

3. _____

Comprehension Check

Underline two problems people had with water in 1787.

MARK the TEXT

Reading Strategy

Circle the main idea of the passage.

MARK the TEXT

Use the Strategy

How did identifying the main idea and details help you understand the passage?

_____

_____

_____

Summarize It!

Summarize the passage for a partner.

_____

_____

_____

_____

Reader's Response

What would you have done about one of the challenges you faced if you lived in Philadelphia in 1787?

_____

_____

_____

Home-School Connection Summarize the passage for a family member.

Name _____ Date _____

Phonics: Consonant Digraphs *ch*, *sh*, and *th*

Use with Student Book page 132.

> The letters *ch*, *sh*, and *th* are called **consonant digraphs**.
> Each consonant digraph stands for one sound. The letters *ch*,
> *sh*, and *th* can be at the beginning, in the middle, or at the
> end of a word.

Find the words with the letters *ch*, *sh*, or *th* in each sentence. Write the words. Then underline *ch*, *sh*, or *th*.

1. She likes to wear matching shoes and shirts.

_____

2. When I am thirsty, I drink chocolate milkshakes.

_____

3. Both merchants are selling shiny children's toys at the fair.

_____

4. I did the wash without my mother's help.

_____

5. If I shoot the ball to the moon, will you catch it?

_____

6. The girls chased seabirds at the seashore.

_____

 **Home-School Connection** Think of five words that have the consonant digraphs *ch, sh*, or *th*.
Write the words. Then read them to a family member.

Comprehension: Main Idea and Details

Use with Student Book pages 134–135.

Read the passage. Circle the main idea. Underline three details.

The Summer Holidays

Summer finally arrived. The Holden family rented a beach house for the month of July. Mr. Holden was really excited because the house was bigger than the one they rented last year. There was enough room in the garage for all of his fishing tackle. He could even fit a boat in there! He was really looking forward to taking his son, Jimmy, deep-sea fishing.

After the family unpacked, they decided to rent a boat. They went to the boat rental place in town that was near the dock. The salesperson asked Mr. Holden what kind of boat he wanted.

"The biggest one you have," Mr. Holden replied. "Make sure the motor works! It would be great to have a refrigerator, too."

"I want a place to put my new fishing tackle," said Jimmy.

Mrs. Holden, Emma, and Ann didn't really care about the boat. They were more interested in renting some blue bikes and exploring shops along the boardwalk. They wanted Jimmy and Mr. Holden to hurry up. They got tired of waiting, so while Jimmy and Mr. Holden spoke with the salesperson, they went to the bike rental shop.

 Have a family member tell or read you a story. (Your family member can use his or her own language.) Identify the main idea and at least one detail in the story.

Name _____ Date _____

Grammar: Letters

Use with Student Book page 136.

When writing a letter:

- Use a capital letter for salutations and closings, street names, names of cities and states, names of months, a person's first and last names, and a person's title.

- Use a comma between the city and state, between the day and the year, and in the greeting and closing.

- Use a period in a person's title.

Read the letter. Correct the punctuation and capitalization.

17 oak street

clearville ny 17804

july 5 2010

dear meg

   I am in Philadelphia for the summer. We're having a great time. Yesterday we went to a museum. Tomorrow, I'm taking the kids on a boating trip down the river. I hope you're having a great summer, too!

   sincerely

   mrs oliver

Write a letter to a friend in another city. Have a family member help you check for correct punctuation and capitalization.

Spelling: Endings -*le*

Use with Student Book page 137.

Read each clue. Then complete the words.

1. something used to sew cloth   need _____

2. opposite of big   lit _____

3. many of us   peo _____

4. a crossword   puz _____

5. not doing anything   id _____

6. something to carry water in   bot _____

7. can do something   ab _____

8. to break into little pieces   crum _____

9. mix up a deck of cards   shuf _____

10. it helps you hold something   han _____

11. holds paper together   stap _____

 Write a message to a friend. Use at least three words with -*le* endings.

_____

_____

 **Think of five more words with -*le* endings. Write your own clue for each word. Share your work with a family member.**

Name _____ Date _____

Vocabulary

Use with Student Book pages 138–139.

Key Words

surrender
veteran
republic
federal
separate
legislature

A. Choose the word that *best* completes each sentence. Write the word.

1. The _____ received a medal for bravery.

2. The _____ government has powers that state governments do not.

3. State laws are made by the _____.

4. A _____ has a government elected by the people.

5. Our enemy waved a white flag to _____.

6. The colonies were _____ from England.

B. Unscramble the words.

7. t e e a v r n   _____

8. r e d f a e l   _____

9. r l e g s i u t e l a   _____

10. s u d r e r r n e   _____

11. p a s e t e r a   _____

12. p u r e b l c i   _____

C. Answer the questions.

13. Why would someone **surrender**?

_____

14. How might a **veteran** be honored?

_____

15. Where does a **legislature** meet?

_____

16. Who is the leader of the **federal** government of the United States?

_____

17. When is a country a **republic**?

_____

18. Why did the colonies **separate** from Britain?

_____

Academic Words

D. Read each sentence. Write a new sentence using the underlined word.

19. Each political party holds a <u>convention</u> so it can elect a representative.

_____

20. The representatives held a <u>debate</u> over the president's new law.

_____

Copyright © by Pearson Education, Inc.

Use each key word in a sentence. Share your sentences with a family member.

Name _____ Date _____

Reader's Companion

Use with Student Book pages 140–145.

One Out of Many

Franklin: Yes. People are afraid of government. They think it will take away their liberty.

Ned: We don't want that!

Bob: Make the government weak!

Franklin: What if we have to fight the British again?

Bob: Didn't they surrender?

Washington: Yes. But they might come back.

Ned: We just need a strong army then.

Franklin: Armies cost money. Yesterday, I saw an army veteran in great need. We must take care of the soldiers who fought in the war. France gave us a loan. We should pay them back. Where will we get the money?

Bob: Oh. Is that the only problem?

Franklin: No! There are many things to figure out. But first, we need a strong federal government.

Washington: But not so strong we lose our freedom. Understand?

Use What You Know

List three fears people had about government in 1787.

1. _____

2. _____

3. _____

Comprehension Check

Circle the text that shows what Washington and Franklin were discussing.
MARK the TEXT

Reading Strategy

MARK the TEXT

What inference can you make about the new U.S. government from this passage? Underline where you found your answer in the text.

_____

_____

_____

Use the Strategy

How did making inferences help you understand the passsage?

_____

_____

_____

Retell It!

Retell this passsage as if you are one of the characters.

_____

_____

_____

_____

Reader's Response

Why do you think it was so difficult to write the U.S. Constitution?

_____

_____

_____

 **Retell the passage to a family member.**

Name _____ Date _____

Word Analysis: Synonyms and Antonyms

Use with Student Book page 146.

> **Synonyms** are words that have the same or similar meanings.
>
> **Antonyms** are words that have opposite meanings.

A. Match each word with its antonym. Write the letter of the correct answer.

1. huge	_____	**a.** weak
2. mean	_____	**b.** old
3. light	_____	**c.** tiny
4. strong	_____	**d.** nice
5. young	_____	**e.** dark

B. Read each word. Then draw a box around its synonym.

6. remove   take off / stick to

7. close   open / shut

8. healthy   ill / well

9. leave   go away / stay

10. begin   start / end

Think of synonyms and antonyms for these words: *short, wet, freezing, soft, furry,* and *sad.* Show your words to a family member.

Comprehension: Make Inferences

Use with Student Book pages 148–149.

Read the passage. Then answer the questions.

Feeding Time

It was 7:00 on Monday morning. All the animals were pacing back and forth in their cages. They always made a lot of noise when Janet came. It was almost as if they were happy to see her. Janet started cutting large slabs of meat. Mabel came over to watch. It was her first day on the job. "It's like this everyday," Janet said. "Same time, same place." Suddenly, there was a loud roar. "Oh dear," Mabel said. "I think Max is tired of waiting!" "Here," Janet said. "Throw this meat into his cage. Be careful, though. Breakfast is his favorite meal!"

1. Where are Janet and Mabel?

_____

_____

2. What are Janet and Mabel doing?

_____

_____

3. How do you know?

_____

_____

Copyright © by Pearson Education, Inc.

Home-School Connection

Have a family member tell or read you a story. (Your family member can use his or her own language.) Talk about the inferences you can make from the story.

Name _____   Date _____

Grammar: Commas in a Series

Use with Student Book page 150.

> **Use a comma to separate each item.**
> **Be sure to use a comma before the conjunction.**

A. Put commas in the sentences.

1. Cows pigs and horses are three of the animals we have on our farm.

2. Mexico Canada and the United States are in North America.

3. The book has pictures on pages 11 12 and 13.

4. Last Saturday we went shopping out to eat and to the movies.

B. Write a sentence for each group of words. Put commas in the right places.

5. apples   grapes   peaches

_____

6. interesting books   funny movies   good music

_____

7. June   July   August

_____

8. to the beach to the mountains to camp

_____

In a book, find examples of commas used in a series. Write out at least two sentences. Make sure you put the commas in the right places. Show your work to a family member.

Spelling: Words with *ght*

Use with Student Book page 151.

Read each clue. Write the word that matches the clue.

SPELLING TIP

Some words have silent letters. In words like **might** and **daughter**, the *gh* is silent. You will have to memorize these words.

bought	caught	daughter
eight	fought	light
night	right	straight
tight		

1. comes after the number *seven* _____

2. opposite of *left* _____

3. past tense of *buy* _____

4. comes after *day* _____

5. opposite of *curved* _____

6. what you get from the *sun* _____

7. past tense of *fight* _____

8. not loose _____

9. female child _____

10. past tense of *catch* _____

 Write a journal entry using at least three of the words in the box.

_____

_____

 Write sentences for five of the words in the box. Share your sentences with a family member.

78

Name _____ Date _____

Review

For use with Student Book pages 106–151.

Answer the questions after reading Unit 3. You can go back and reread to help find the answers.

1. In *Writing a Great Speech,* what does the British crown refer to? Circle the letter of the correct answer.

    a. the top of your head   **c.** the king and the government

    b. a cover for a broken tooth   **d.** jewelry worn on the head

2. What are three things a good speech should have?

_____

_____

3. Write the name of one great American speaker. Why is the speaker great?

_____

_____

4. How was the weather described in *One Hot Summer in Philadelphia*? Circle the letter of the correct answer.

    a. hot and humid   **c.** snowy and windy

    b. cold and rainy   **d.** dry and crisp

5. What kinds of people lived and worked in Philadelphia in 1787?

_____

_____

6. What does the title *One Out of Many* mean? Explain.

_____

_____

7. What is a *republic*? Circle the letter of the correct answer.

    a. a kind of political party

    b. a government led by a king

    c. a large group of buildings

    d. a government led by the people

8. Complete a 5 W Chart for *One Out of Many.* Have a partner help you write answers to your questions.

5 W	Questions	Answers
Who?		
What?		
Where?		
When?		
Why?		

Tell a family member something new you learned in this unit.

Name _____ Date _____

Vocabulary

Use with Student Book pages 166–167.

A. Choose the word that *best* completes each sentence. Write the word.

1. An area that is very hot and very wet is

said to be _____.

2. The soil in the _____ is
frozen most of the year.

3. The imaginary line around the middle of Earth is the

_____.

4. An area of land that receives very little rain is a

_____.

5. The great quantity of salt water that covers most of Earth is the

_____.

6. A large area characterized by specific plants and animals is a

_____.

7. _____ are large areas where many grasses,
but few trees, grow.

B. **Answer the questions.**

8. How are a **tropical** rain forest and a **desert** different?

_____

9. How would you describe the **tundra** in winter?

_____

10. What animals live on **grasslands**?

_____

11. What **ocean** can you find below the **equator**?

_____

12. Which **biome** do you live in?

_____

Academic Words

C. **Read each sentence. Write a new sentence using the underlined word.**

13. One way plants <u>adapt</u> to the desert is to grow very long roots.

_____

14. Scientists <u>classify</u> plants and animals on Earth into different kingdoms.

_____

Use each key word in a sentence. Share your sentences with a family member.

Name _____ Date _____

Reader's Companion

Use with Student Book pages 168–175.

Biomes All Over the World

The arctic tundra is the coldest biome on Earth. Trees do not grow in the tundra. Winds are very strong. Ice covers the ground, and water freezes. Animals such as polar bears must be able to live in the cold. Most animals that live in the tundra have extra fat to keep them warm. Many birds and other animals migrate, or move, to a warmer climate for the winter.

In the summer, the weather is warm enough in the tundra for things to grow. Plants and flowers appear. These plants and flowers can live in colder temperatures. Animals that eat plants and grass can find more food during the summer.

Use What You Know

List three animals that might live in the tundra.

1. _____
2. _____
3. _____

Comprehension Check

MARK the TEXT

Underline the parts of the passage that tell you how animals live in the tundra.

Reading Strategy

MARK the TEXT

Describe an animal that might live in the tundra. Circle words in the passage that helped you visualize the animal.

_____

_____

_____

Use the Strategy

How did visualizing help you understand the passage?

_____

_____

_____

Summarize It!

Summarize the passage for a partner.

_____

_____

_____

_____

Reader's Response

Would you want to visit the tundra? Why or why not?

_____

_____

_____

Summarize the passage for a family member.

Name _____ Date _____

Phonics: Final /s/ and /z/ sounds

Use with Student Book page 176.

> Voiceless *s* sounds like a snake hissing, *sssss*. Voiced *s* sounds like *z*. Think of the sound a bee makes, *buzzzz*.

Read each word. Write if the final *s* sounds like a snake or like a bee. Write *s* or *z* to indicate the sound.

1. pages _____

2. laughs _____

3. hugs _____

4. mixes _____

5. hotels _____

6. eggs _____

7. sings _____

8. boxes _____

9. talks _____

10. calls _____

11. laughs _____

12. learns _____

13. cats _____

14. tries _____

 Think of five more words with the final /s/ sound. Practice saying the words correctly with a family member.

Comprehension: Visualize

Use with Student Book pages 178–179.

Read each passage. Write the words and phrases that helped you form a mental picture of the passage.

The Tundra

1. It is winter in the tundra. An arctic hare sits in the snow. The strong, cold wind blows all around it. The artic hare's white fur coat and a layer of fat keep it warm. The hare's large feet help it stay on top of the snow. Suddenly, the hare is on the move. It darts below the snow, into its den.

_____

_____

Trees in the Rain Forest

2. The Amazon River winds through parts of South America. Most of the land around the river is tropical rain forest. Trees in this rain forest grow as tall as 200 feet! These huge trees need a lot of good soil to grow. Everything a tree needs to grow strong and tall is in the top layer of soil on the forest floor. Roots grow above or near the surface. The roots of rain forest trees spread out from the trunk.

_____

_____

Have a family member read or tell you a story. (The family member can use his or her own language.) Write what you visualize from the story and share it with the class.

Name _____ Date _____

Grammar: Conjunctions and Transitions

Use with Student Book page 180.

> **Conjunctions** join two related sentences together to form a compound sentence.
>
> **Transitions** show a change in ideas from one sentence to another.

A. Read each sentence. Underline *and* or *but* when they are used as conjunctions. Draw a box around *and* or *but* when they are used to form transitions.

1. Plants live on land, and they also grow underwater.

2. Many animals eat only plants. But some animals eat only other animals.

3. Dolphins swim in groups. And they are one of the few mammals that live in water.

4. Starfish live in water, but they aren't really fish.

B. Write the word *and* or *but* to complete each sentence. Then write Conjunction or Transition to show how they are used.

5. Zebras are members of the horse family, _____ they look very

   different from horses. _____

6. Some animals graze on grass, _____ others eat leaves from

   bushes. _____

Find two examples of conjunctions or transitions in a newspaper or book. Show your examples to a family member.

Spelling: Consonant Clusters *ch* and *tch*

Use with Student Book page 181.

Read each clue. Write the word that matches the clue.

beach	bench
match	peach
pitch	sandwich
scratch	

SPELLING TIP

When a one-syllable word ends with a short vowel and the /ch/ sound, that sound is spelled *ch* or *tch*. Check a dictionary to get the correct spelling.

1. a small cut _____

2. two of a kind _____

3. you sit on it at the park _____

4. you eat this at lunch _____

5. a pretty color or a type of fruit _____

6. a fun place to be in the summer _____

7. to throw a baseball _____

 Write a journal entry using at least four of the words in the box.

_____

_____

_____

 **Use a dictionary to find the definitions of three of the words. Show your definitions to a family member.**

Name _____ Date _____

Vocabulary
Use with Student Book pages 182–183.

Key Words

pods
orphan
migrated
predator
reunite
starvation

A. Choose the word that *best* completes each sentence. Write the word.

1. Orcas live in _____.

2. Rabbits know a coyote

is a _____.

3. The baby deer became an

_____ when its mother died.

4. Scientists wanted to _____ Springer with her pod.

5. Some of the birds _____ south.

6. Suffering or dying from hunger is _____.

B. Match each word with its definition. Write the letter of the correct answer.

7. predator _____ **a.** moved to another area

8. pods _____ **b.** a person or animal without parents

9. starvation _____ **c.** an animal that hunts another animal for food

10. orphan _____ **d.** a family group of animals that live in the sea

11. migrated _____ **e.** to bring together again

12. reunite _____ **f.** suffering or death from lack of food

89

C. Answer the questions.

13. What makes an animal an **orphan**?

_____

14. Why is it difficult to **reunite** sea mammals with their **pods**?

_____

15. When the birds **migrated**, where did they go?

_____

16. How might an animal avoid **starvation**?

_____

17. What animal is a **predator**?

_____

Academic Words

D. Read each sentence. Write a new sentence using the underlined word.

18. An adult elephant can <u>consume</u> about 400 pounds of grass and leaves every day.

_____

19. The scientists' <u>goal</u> was to return Springer to her pod.

_____

 Use each key word in a sentence. Share your sentences with a family member.

Copyright © by Pearson Education, Inc.

Name _____ Date _____

Reader's Companion

Use with Student Book pages 184–187.

Springer Goes Home

People traveling to work on the ferry in Puget Sound, near Seattle, Washington, got a surprise one morning in 2002. A baby orca was swimming alone in the water. Orcas are sometimes called killer whales. They are not whales at all. They are dolphins.

People were delighted to watch the baby orca. She played with floating logs and rubbed against boats. They called her Springer. Scientists gave her the name A-73. They were very concerned. Orcas live in family groups called pods. It is rare to see an orca traveling alone. Scientists also worried about Springer's smell because they thought she might be starving to death. Mammals, like Springer, sometimes have bad breath when they are breaking down their own body fat instead of eating.

Scientists could tell which pod Springer belonged to by the sounds she made. The scientists believed Springer's mother died in 2000, leaving her an orphan.

Use What You Know

List three reasons why scientists were worried about Springer.

1. _____

2. _____

3. _____

Genre

MARK the TEXT

Underline the parts of the passage that gave you information about why Springer was swimming alone.

Comprehension Check

MARK the TEXT

How did scientists know which pod Springer belonged to? Circle the parts of the passage where you found your answer.

91

Use the Strategy

How did making predictions help you understand the passage?

_____

_____

_____

Summarize It!

Summarize the passage for a partner.

_____

_____

_____

_____

Reader's Response

Should people help orphaned animals? Why or why not?

_____

_____

_____

Summarize the passage for a family member.

Name _____   Date _____

Phonics: Consonant Clusters

Use with Student Book page 188.

When *r*, *l*, or *s* come together with another consonant at the beginning of the word, the sounds of both letters usually blend together.

bluefish	breathing	close	freshwater
glide	~~place~~	~~predator~~	~~small~~
snap	spout	swim	trouble

A. Write each word from the box in the correct column.

r- blends	*s*- blends	*l*- blends
predator	small	place
_____	_____	_____
_____	_____	_____
_____	_____	_____

B. Read each clue. Write a consonant cluster that completes each word.

1. the color of grass ___ ___ e e n

2. animal with a soft body and an outer shell ___ ___ a i l

3. round, puffy shapes in the sky ___ ___ o u d s

4. a big, black bird ___ ___ o w

 **Add two more words to each column of the chart. Share your words with a family member.**

Comprehension: Problem and Solution

For use with Student Book pages 190–191.

Read the passage. Identify the problem in the passage. Come up with a possible solution.

Where's the Goalie?

I go to a very small school. The school is so small that there are exactly 11 players on our soccer team. José is our goalie. He works very hard to keep the other team from scoring goals. He is the best goalie ever! My team has a very important game today. It is the final game of the season. José is sick. He has a very bad cold. His mother told him to stay in bed today. What can we do?

1. What is the problem?

_____

_____

2. What are some possible solutions to the problem?

_____

_____

3. Which solution would you choose? Why?

_____

_____

_____

Have a family member read or tell you a story. (The family member can use his or her own language.) Talk about the problems and solutions in the story. Share what you learned with the class.

Name _____ Date _____

Grammar: Complete and Incomplete Sentences

Use with Student Book page 192.

> A **complete sentence** expresses a complete thought. It begins with a capital letter and ends with a period.
>
> **Complete sentence:** The weather is hot.
>
> **Incomplete sentence:** hot weather

A. Unscramble the words to write a complete sentence.

1. called killer orcas whales are _____

2. ride boat short is the _____

3. study things scientists living _____

4. food live animals to need _____

5. breathe whales air dolphins and _____

B. Write a complete sentence for each group of words.

6. in the ocean _____

7. the orphan monkey _____

8. migrate south _____

9. see many things _____

10. every summer _____

 Write three more complete sentences on any subject. Share your sentences with a family member.

95

Spelling: Adding *-ed* or *-ing* to Verbs

Use with Student Book page 193.

Make new words by adding *-ed* or *-ing*. The first one is done for you.

SPELLING TIP

You can simply add *-ed* or *-ing* to many one-syllable verbs. However, with some one-syllable verbs, you will need to double the final consonant, as in *swimming.*

1. drop

add *-ed* _____dropped_____

add *-ing* _____

2. watch

add *-ed* _____

add *-ing* _____

3. grab

add *-ed* _____

add *-ing* _____

4. snow

add *-ed* _____

add *-ing* _____

Write a short paragraph that uses three words with *-ed* or *-ing* endings.

_____

_____

_____

Home-School Connection Think of five more words that have the *-ed/-ing* pattern. Write each form of the words. Show your work to a family member.

Name _____ Date _____

Vocabulary

Use with Student Book pages 194–195.

Key Words

assistance
handle
damage
stranded
relief

A. **Choose the word that *best* completes each sentence. Write the word.**

1. The fire caused a lot of _____ .

2. There were plenty of helpers to

   _____ the job.

3. We were given food and shelter at the _____ center.

4. The snowstorm left us _____ on the mountain.

5. Rescue workers gave _____ to those who needed it.

B. **Read each clue. Circle the key word in the row of letters. Then write the word.**

6. to be stuck in one place _____ daretastranded

7. take care of or manage _____ khandlehible

8. help _____ seacassistancenasi

9. money, food, or clothing _____ pedreliefcot

10. change for the worse, break _____ weiiybdamagewtyb

97

C. Answer the questions.

11. Who gives **assistance** during an emergency?

_____

12. Where could a person get **stranded**?

_____

13. What **damage** can a hurricane cause?

_____

14. How do workers **handle** an emergency?

_____

15. What kinds of **relief** supplies are needed in a disaster?

_____

Academic Words

D. Read each sentence. Write a new sentence using the underlined word.

16. The volunteers were told to wait for instructions from the <u>authorities</u>.

_____

17. Volunteers worked hard to <u>establish</u> a relief center after the hurricane.

_____

Copyright © by Pearson Education, Inc.

Use each key word in a sentence. Share your sentences with a family member.

Name _____ Date _____

Reader's Companion

Use with Student Book pages 196–201.

After the Hurricane

After a hurricane, experts come and assess the towns that were damaged. They call rescue workers to help. They also let others know when more help is needed. People come from nearby and far away to give relief to those who need it. These people are usually volunteers. They do not get paid for their work. They come because they know that people need help after a hurricane.

Many people lose their homes during hurricanes. These people need to stay someplace, such as a shelter, until they can go home. They might feel sad and scared. Volunteers work to help these people feel better. The volunteers can play with children. They can help people find missing friends or family. Sometimes, people just need to talk to someone about what happened.

Use What You Know

Make a list of bad weather events.

1. _____

2. _____

3. _____

Comprehension Check

MARK the TEXT

How do volunteers help after a hurricane? Underline the parts of the passage where you found your answer.

Reading Strategy

MARK the TEXT

Write a question about the passage. Circle the parts of the passage where you found the answer.

_____

_____

Use the Strategy

How did asking questions help you understand the passage?

_____

_____

_____

Summarize It!

Summarize the passage as if you are a relief volunteer.

_____

_____

_____

_____

Reader's Response

Describe one way you can volunteer to help after a disaster.

_____

_____

_____

Summarize the passage for a family member.

Name _____ Date _____

Word Analysis: Homophones

Use with Student Book page 202.

> Words that sound the same but have different
> spellings and meanings are **homophones**.

**Read each clue. Circle the correct homophone for each sentence.
Then write the word.**

1. Clue: Which word means *a single thing*?

_____ river went over its bank. (Won, One)

2. Clue: Which word means *caused to go*?

A boat was _____ to rescue us. (sent, cent)

3. Clue: Which word means *listened with your ears*?

We _____ the boat horn honking. (herd, heard)

4. Clue: Which word means *belonging to us*?

The rescuers asked us _____ names. (our, hour)

5. Clue: Which word means *body around which Earth revolves*?

The _____ was still out, so we had plenty of
light. (sun, son)

6. Clue: Which word means *part of a plant*?

Each _____ was red and yellow. (flour, flower)

Think of another pair of homophones. Use each word in a
sentence. Show your sentences to a family member.

Comprehension: Sequence

Use with Student Book pages 204–205.

Read the passage. Answer the questions.

Here Comes the Hurricane

The newscaster said a hurricane would hit our area in a few days. First, Mom and my sister went to the store to buy extra food, water, batteries, and other items. Next, Dad and I put the supplies Mom and my sister bought in a waterproof container. Later, Dad and the neighbors helped each other board up windows. Finally, the hurricane came. Mom, Dad, my sister, our dog, and I went to the safest place in the house. We listened to the radio until the newscaster said the hurricane had passed. After the hurricane was over, we went outside to assess the damage.

1. Write the sequence words you find in the passage.

_____

_____

_____

2. Can you think of something else the family should have done? Where do you think it could go in the sequence?

_____

_____

_____

 **Write a sequence of events to describe a chore you do at home. Share your work with a family member.**

Name _____   Date _____

Grammar: Prepositions

Use with Student Book page 206.

> **Prepositions** link words in a sentence. Prepositions show *when, where,* or *how* two things are connected.

A. Read each sentence. Circle the preposition(s). Some sentences have more than one preposition. Then write the word(s).

1. A tornado came through town. _____

2. We moved into the basement during the storm.

   _____

3. The wind blew across the fields. _____

4. The tornado moved toward the west. _____

5. After the storm, we went to the shelter. _____

B. Complete each sentence with the correct preposition. Write the word.

6. The highway was damaged _____ the flood. (for, by)

7. Animals ran _____ the fire. (with, from)

8. Special airplanes poured water _____ the trees. (during, over)

9. Stay out of the forest _____ it is safe. (until, over)

 Write sentences with the prepositions *for, without, upon,* and *near.* Share your sentences with a family member.

Spelling: Homophones

Use with Student Book page 207.

Complete each sentence with the correct homophone.

SPELLING
TIP

Learn the homophones for common words. Always check your writing to make sure you have used the correct word.

1. ate   eight

My brother is _____ years old.

He _____ everything on his plate.

2. one   won

She had trouble spelling _____ of the words.

I _____ the spelling bee!

3. to   two   too

Kai needs a map _____ the beach.

I want to go, _____ .

He is taking his _____ cousins.

  Write a journal entry using homophones. Underline the words that are homophones.

_____

_____

_____

 Write definitions for the words in two homophone pairs. Share your definitions with a family member.

Name _____ Date _____

Review

Use with Student Book pages 160–207.

Answer the questions after reading Unit 4. You can go back and reread to help find the answers.

1. Refer to *Biomes All Over the World*. Compare and contrast how mountains and tundras are similar and different.

How Mountains and Tundras Are Similar	How Mountains and Tundras Are Different

2. Which words best describe a *tropical* climate? Circle the letter of the correct answer.

    a. cold and dry   **c.** hot and dry

    b. hot and humid   **d.** covered with water

3. Why are oceans important?

_____

_____

_____

4. In *Springer Goes Home*, what kind of animal is Springer? Circle the letter of the correct answer.

    a. insect   **c.** fish

    b. orca   **d.** bird

5. Which of the following was NOT an option scientists considered for Springer? Circle the letter of the correct answer.

    a. let nature take its course
    b. take her to a marine park
    c. find another pod for her
    d. return her to her own pod

6. Where did scientists find Springer at the end of the selection?

_____

_____

_____

7. According to *After the Hurricane*, where do hurricanes form? Circle the letter of the correct answer.

    a. over the mountains   **c.** over deserts
    b. over the ocean   **d.** over the tundra

8. What can volunteers do to help after a hurricane?

_____

_____

_____

9. Write one question you would like to ask about *After the Hurricane*.

_____

Tell a family member something new you learned in this unit.

Name _____ Date _____

Vocabulary

Use with Student Book pages 220–221.

A. Choose the word that *best* fits each definition. Write the word.

Key Words

musicians
instruments
percussion
sounds
vibrations
hearing

1. objects used for making musical sounds

_____

2. something you experience by hearing

_____

3. people who play musical instruments _____

4. the sense you use to listen to music _____

5. continuous shaking movements _____

6. instruments that make sounds when they are hit

_____

B. Choose the word that *best* completes each sentence. Write the word.

7. Drums and cymbals are different _____ instruments.

8. I can play many different _____, but Eva can only play the saxophone.

9. Some _____ play in marching bands.

10. You can both hear and feel _____.

11. My dad listened closely because his _____ is not good.

12. _____ travel through the air to my ear.

C. Answer the questions.

13. Who are some of your favorite **musicians**?

_____

14. What **instruments** play your favorite **sounds**?

_____

15. How do you play **percussion** instruments?

_____

16. Which objects make **vibrations**?

_____

17. How can people who have lost their **hearing** hear sounds?

_____

Academic Words

D. Read each sentence. Write a new sentence using the underlined word.

18. The students took the principal's joke out of <u>context</u> and became very angry.

_____

19. Evelyn will <u>demonstrate</u> how to play the marimbas.

_____

 **Use each key word in a sentence. Share your sentences with a family member.**

Name _____ Date _____

Reader's Companion

Use with Student Book pages 222–225.

Touching Sound with Evelyn Glennie

Evelyn grew up on a farm in Scotland. There was a piano in her home. As a young child, she asked her parents to let her take piano lessons. They let her take lessons when she was eight years old. Evelyn soon found out she had what musicians call "perfect pitch." She could hear the notes perfectly in her mind. This was good, because she was slowly losing her hearing.

Evelyn found that hearing aids kept her from being able to perceive sounds with the rest of her body. She stopped wearing them when she was 12 years old. Evelyn knew she could hear the correct music notes in her mind. She also used her body to feel the vibrations the instruments made. She learned to play many percussion instruments. This surprised her teachers, who thought Evelyn would not be able to play music once she lost her hearing.

Use What You Know

List three parts of your body where you can perceive sounds.

1. _____

2. _____

3. _____

Comprehension Check

Draw a circle around three details in the passage. 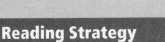 MARK the TEXT

Reading Strategy

What is the main idea of this passage? Underline where you found the answer. MARK the TEXT

Use the Strategy

How did identifying the main idea and details help you understand the passage?

_____

_____

_____

Summarize It!

Summarize the passage for a partner.

_____

_____

_____

Reader's Response

Which percussion instrument(s) do you like best? Why?

_____

_____

_____

Copyright © by Pearson Education, Inc.

Summarize the passage for a family member.

Name _____   Date _____

Phonics: Ending -*ed*

Use with Student Book page 226.

> If the letter *d* or the letter *t* comes before the -*ed*
> ending, then -*ed* is pronounced as a separate syllable.

Write each verb in the correct column of the chart. The first one is done for you.

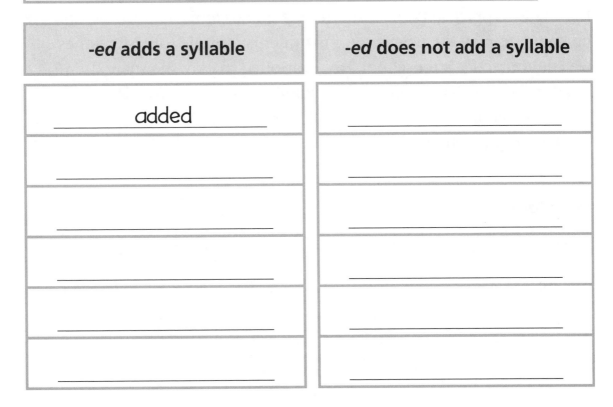

added	constructed	flapped	grated
greeted	opened	started	stayed
stopped	traded	watered	worked

-*ed* adds a syllable	-*ed* does not add a syllable
added	

 **Home-School Connection** Find verbs with the -*ed* ending in a magazine or newspaper.
Show your examples to a family member.

Comprehension: Main Idea and Details

Use with Student Book pages 228–229.

Read the passage. Write the main idea and three details.

The Percussion Section

Mrs. Jones, the music teacher, put an announcement on the school bulletin board. She was holding auditions for the orchestra. My friends and I were so excited. We asked Mrs. Jones what kinds of players she was looking for. She said she really needed people to play percussion instruments. She said it was hard to get people to play percussion instruments because the players had to stand at the back of the orchestra to play. Also, the instruments were very loud, so parents didn't want their kids to practice them at home. My friends and I said we would be happy to play the percussion instruments. Ronnie told Mrs. Jones we could practice after school. He auditioned to play the snare drum. I auditioned to play the bass drum. Juanita auditioned to play the triangles, cymbals, and rattles. Mrs. Jones was very happy. "Now we can have a full orchestra," she said.

Main Idea: _____

Detail: _____

Detail: _____

Detail: _____

Have a family member read or tell you a story. (The family member can use his or her own language.) Tell your family member the main idea and three details from the story.

Name _____ Date _____

Grammar and Writing:

Appositives and Prepositional Phrases

Use with Student Book pages 230–231.

> An **appositive** is a noun or noun phrase that describes another noun.
>
> A **prepositional phrase** tells about a noun or pronoun in a sentence. Prepositional phrases can include prepositions like *on*, *above*, *over*, *under*, *in*, *before*, and *during*.

Underline the appositive. Draw a box around the prepositional phrase and a line through the preposition. Not all of the sentences have an appositive.

1. My friend, <u>Anish</u>, jumped over the fence .

2. There is a beautiful garden behind the house.

3. Denver, the capital of Colorado, is the home of the Denver Broncos.

4. Andy Magic, a professional magician, was the star of the show.

5. Maria found her doll in the big, messy pile of toys.

6. Susan's baby sister, Mary Ellen, will be four years old in June.

7. We sang and laughed during the whole trip.

8. After school, I took my cousin, Enrique, to the park.

9. We saw a great movie at the cinema.

10. My friend, Susan, told me about the instruments.

Write a short paragraph about a game you played with a group of friends. Underline the appositives and draw a box around the prepositional phrases you use. Share your work with a family member.

Spelling: Finding Related Words

Use with Student Book page 231.

Read each word. Write the smaller word found in it.

1. performance _____

2. climber _____

3. anchored _____

4. mixture _____

5. graphic _____

6. soloist _____

7. oily _____

8. throughout _____

9. musical _____

10. wonderful _____

 Write a journal entry using at least four of the words above.

_____

_____

_____

 Find five words that contain a related word in a newspaper or magazine. Show your words to a family member.

Name _____ Date _____

Vocabulary

Use with Student Book pages 232–233.

Key Words

code
escape
landmarks
secret
riverbank
tracks

A. Choose the word that *best* completes each sentence. Write the word.

1. The statues in town are _____.

2. When you get away from something, you

_____.

3. The edge of a river is a _____.

4. Your footprints in the sand can also be called

_____.

5. Something you know that you keep others from knowing is a

_____.

6. A _____ is a group of words, phrases, or symbols that has a special meaning.

B. Read the pairs of sentences. One makes sense. The other is silly. Write an S next to each sentence that makes sense. Write an X next to each silly sentence.

7. A river has two <u>riverbanks</u>. _____

A river has ten <u>riverbanks</u>. _____

8. You can find the horse by following its <u>tracks</u>. _____

You can lose the horse by following its <u>tracks</u>. _____

C. Answer the questions.

9. When might people use a **code** to communicate?

_____

10. What are some things people might want to **escape**?

_____

11. What are some **landmarks** where you live?

_____

12. What things do people want to keep **secret**?

_____

13. What might you do on a **riverbank**?

_____

14. Where can you find animal **tracks**?

_____

Academic Words

D. Read each sentence. Write a new sentence using the underlined word.

15. It was nice of Khalifa to <u>assist</u> me with my homework.

_____

16. My sister, Lisa, said she would <u>accompany</u> me to the audition.

_____

Use each key word in a sentence. Share your sentences with a family member.

Name _____ Date _____

Reader's Companion

Use with Student Book pages 234–237.

A Song Map

Who was the old man waiting to carry them to freedom? Some people believe he was Peg Leg Joe, a former sailor who helped slaves. Peg Leg Joe used a wooden leg.

Chorus
Follow the drinking gourd!
Follow the drinking gourd!
For the old man is waiting for to carry you to freedom
If you follow the drinking gourd.

Stanza 2
The riverbank makes a very good road,
The dead trees will show you the way,
Left foot, peg foot traveling on,
Following the drinking gourd.

Some people say Peg Leg Joe marked trees and other landmarks along the riverbank. This helped the slaves make sure they were going in the right direction. These tracks, or marks, were often a mud or charcoal outline of a human left foot and another mark. Some people believe the other mark was Peg Leg Joe's wooden leg.

Use What You Know

List three things a secret code might have.

1. _____

2. _____

3. _____

Comprehension Check

Underline the directions given in Stanza 2.

MARK the TEXT

Genre

MARK the TEXT

What marks did Peg Leg Joe leave? Circle the text where you found your response.

Use the Strategy

How did summarizing help you understand the passage?

_____

_____

_____

Summarize It!

Summarize the directions for a partner.

_____

_____

_____

_____

Reader's Response

What other kinds of messages can you find in songs?

_____

_____

_____

Home-School Connection Summarize the passage for a family member.

Name _____ Date _____

Word Analysis: Figurative Language

Use with Student Book page 238.

> Writers sometimes use **figurative language**
> to paint word pictures.

**Read each sentence. Underline the figurative language in each
sentence. Then write what you think it means.**

1. The volcano <u>coughed rock and ash</u>.

The volcano erupted.

2. Her smile lit up my heart.

_____

3. The breeze whispered through the leaves.

_____

4. I ate so much that I'm going to explode.

_____

5. All the trees bowed with respect to the wind.

_____

6. His mouth runs like a motor.

_____

7. Her eyes sparkled like stars.

_____

8. Xiao can run like the wind.

_____

Comprehension: Make Inferences

Use with Student Book pages 240–241.

Read the passage. Answer the questions.

Landmarks

Have you ever seen a landmark? You probably have. Landmarks are everywhere! People like to visit these important places. Some landmarks honor important people from the past. Are there any statues in your town? Statues can also be landmarks. Many landmarks tell about the history of a place. The Statue of Liberty is an important landmark. It tells about the history of New York and the United States. The Gateway Arch in Missouri and The Alamo in Texas are two other important American landmarks. What landmarks do you have in your town?

1. What is this passage about?

_____

2. What do landmarks represent?

_____

3. Why do people like to visit landmarks?

_____

4. How does something become a landmark?

_____

Listen to a song with a family member. The song can be in your own language. Discuss an inference you can make from the song with the family member.

Name _____ Date _____

Grammar and Writing:

Dependent and Independent Clauses

Use with Student Book pages 242–243.

> An **independent clause** has a subject and a predicate
> (verb) and can stand alone as a sentence. A **dependent
> clause** has a subject and verb, but it cannot stand alone
> as a sentence.

**Read each sentence. Write whether the underlined words
are independent or dependent clauses.**

1. <u>We saw your sister</u> at the park after school.

_____

2. Mario used to take the bus <u>before he bought his car</u>.

_____

3. I always put the clock on the table <u>since it is next to my bed</u>.

_____

4. If you look closely, <u>you'll see animal tracks in the snow</u>.

_____

5. Mom likes our new house <u>because it is big</u>.

_____

6. <u>They live near the landmark</u> on Main Street.

_____

 **Find five examples of independent or dependent clauses in a magazine
or newspaper article. Show your work to a family member.**

Spelling: /j/ Sound Spelled with *g*

Use with Student Book page 243.

gem	general	generous
genius	geography	giant
ginger	giraffe	

Read each clue. Write the word that matches the clue.

1. an animal with a long neck _____

2. a very smart person _____

3. huge, very big _____

4. a jewel or precious stone _____

5. a spice _____

6. only the main features of something _____

7. willing to give time or money to another _____

8. study of the countries of the world _____

 Write a paragraph using at least four words that have the /j/ sound spelled with *g*. You can choose words from the box above.

_____

_____

_____

 Write the meanings of four words with the /j/ sound spelled with *g*. Share your work with a family member.

Name _____ Date _____

Vocabulary

Use with Student Book pages 244–245.

Key Words

rhythms
kazoo
harmonies
flea market
improvisation

A. Choose the word that *best* fits each definition. Write the word.

1. instruments, notes, or voices that sound

   good together _____

2. music performed without any preparation

   _____

3. repeated patterns of sounds in music or speech

   _____

4. a market where old or used goods are sold

   _____

5. an instrument that creates a buzzing quality to the human voice

   _____

B. Read each clue. Find the key word in the row of letters. Then circle the word.

6. a toy and a musical instrument   oupoupoukazoooouiyioy

7. an unplanned performance   eietihvbimprovisationbceubcv

8. repeating pattern of
   movements or sounds   hgvbevbrhythmsvrnvo

C. Answer the questions.

9. What types of music use **improvisation**?

_____

10. What does a **kazoo** sound like?

_____

11. What kinds of things might you find at a **flea market**?

_____

12. What kinds of instruments play **rhythms**?

_____

13. Who or what performs **harmonies**?

_____

Academic Words

D. Read each sentence. Write a new sentence using the underlined word.

14. The music we had to play had a lot of <u>complexity</u>.

_____

15. The orchestra had a <u>variety</u> of instruments.

_____

Use each key word in a sentence. Share your sentences with a family member.

Name _____ Date _____

Reader's Companion

Use with Student Book pages 246–251.

Homemade Music

A washboard is a piece of metal with ridges. Many years ago, people used washboards to wash clothes. The ridges helped to get out the dirt. Now, people play music on washboards. You can stroke the ridges with almost anything. Some players use thimbles. Other players use wooden spoons, can openers, or their fingers. Each object will make a different sound. If you go to a local flea market, you may find a washboard!

You have your instruments. Your band is ready to go! Have each of your friends pick an instrument. Let them practice on their own. Then get together and play. Now it is time for some improvisation. Improvisation can also be called jamming. Jam with your friends on your homemade instruments!

Use What You Know

List three objects you can make into homemade instruments.

1. _____

2. _____

3. _____

Comprehension Check

Where can you find a washboard? How do people play them? Underline the parts of the passage where you found your answers.

MARK the TEXT

Genre

MARK the TEXT

Circle the part of the passage that explains what a washboard is.

Use the Strategy

Why is it helpful to identify the author's purpose as you read?

_____

_____

_____

Summarize It!

Summarize the passage for a partner.

_____

_____

_____

_____

Reader's Response

What is your favorite homemade musical instrument? Why?

_____

_____

_____

 **Summarize the passage for a family member.**

Name _____ Date _____

Phonics: Words with *ow, ou*

Use with Student Book page 252.

> The diphthong /*ou*/ can be spelled as either *ou* or *ow*.
> Sometimes ow can make a long *o* sound. If one sound
> doesn't make sense, try the other.

**Read each clue. Fill in the blank with vowels to complete the word.
Practice saying each word with a partner.**

1. move a ball up and down   b _____ nce

2. a lot of people in one place   cr _____ d

3. do this in a boat   r _____

4. opposite of up   d _____ n

5. something you might live in   h _____ se

6. not to lead, but to   foll _____

7. a person, place, or thing   n _____ n

8. a king or queen wears this   cr _____ n

9. a cat likes to chase one   m _____ se

10. covers the ground in winter   sn _____

Home-School Connection Look through a newspaper or magazine. Find six more words that are spelled with *ou* or *ow*. Show your words to a family member.

Comprehension: Author's Purpose

Use with Student Book pages 254–255.

Read the passage. Answer the questions.

Join the Eagletown Marching Band

Have you ever wanted to make music? Would you like to march in parades? Do you dream of performing in a large stadium? This is your big chance! Don't worry! You don't have to be a great musician. We will even teach you how to play an instrument. The Eagletown Marching Band needs drum players and horn players. We even need a few people to play the kazoo! What do you have to do? Just come to the tryouts this Saturday at the high school. We'll be there from noon until five o'clock. If you want to meet new people and have a great time, come and join the Eagletown Marching Band!

1. What is the author's purpose?

_____

_____

2. Explain how you found your answer.

_____

_____

3. How did identifying the author's purpose help you understand the text?

_____

_____

 **Read a newspaper or magazine article with a family member. Tell a family member about the author's purpose.**

Name _____ Date _____

Grammar: Commonly Misused Words

Use with Student Book page 256.

lay/lie	raise/rise	set/sit

**Complete each sentence with the correct word.
Some examples have more than one choice.**

1. Will you please _____ the table?

2. _____ the cards on the table.

3. _____ in that chair, please.

4. To make bread, you need to let the dough

_____ .

5. Would you like to _____ on the couch?

6. Go outside and _____ the flag.

7. Everyone should _____ when the judge enters
the courtroom.

8. It is important to let the glue _____ before
using the toy.

9. Would you please _____ the packages on
the floor?

10. It is wonderful to watch the sun _____ .

 **Pick one pair of words from the box. Write a sentence for each
word. Share your work with a family member.**

Spelling: Words with Silent Letters

Use with Student Book page 257.

SPELLING TIP

Learn to spell words with silent letters and hard spellings by saying them aloud exactly as they are spelled.

Say each word including the silent letter. Then use each word in a sentence. The first one is done for you.

1. wrist   wuh-rist   My sister broke her wrist.

2. knee   kuh-nee   _____

3. handsome   hand-sum   _____

4. ghost   guh-host   _____

5. often   off-ten   _____

6. island   i-sland   _____

7. toward   to-ward   _____

8. soften   sof-ten   _____

Write a journal entry using at least three words with silent letters. Show your work to a partner.

_____

_____

_____

 **Make a list of five more words with silent letters. Show your list to a family member.**

Name _____ Date _____

Review

Use with Student Book pages 214–257.

Answer the questions after reading Unit 5. You can go back and reread to help find the answers.

1. In *Touching Sound with Evelyn Glennie*, what instrument did Evelyn play in New York City's Grand Central Station? Circle the letter of the correct answer.

    a. marimba   **c.** snare drum

    b. xylophone   **d.** washboard

2. "Evelyn soon found out she had what musicians call 'perfect pitch'." Perfect pitch is

    a. the ability to copy notes someone else plays or sings.

    b. the ability to hear notes perfectly in one's mind.

    c. the ability to play any instrument without lessons.

    d. the ability to perceive music in other parts of the body.

3. What do you think the film title *Touch the Sound* means?

_____

_____

4. In *A Song Map*, what is believed to be the *drinking gourd*? Circle the letter of the correct answer.

    a. kind of squash   **c.** the Big Dipper

    b. type of ladle   **d.** type of tea kettle

5. Who was Peg Leg Joe?

_____

_____

6. Use the Inference Chart below to interpret one of the verses of
Follow the Drinking Gourd. Follow the example.

Verse	What I Know	Inference
When the sun comes back and the first quail calls...	The slaves had to cross a large river.	It was easier to cross the river in winter.

7. What was the author's purpose in writing *Homemade Music?* Circle
the letter of the correct answer.

   a. to entertain

   b. to inform

   c. to persuade

8. Describe in your own words how to make jingle bracelets.

_____

_____

_____

9. Improvisation is also called

   a. performing

   b. adapting

   c. jamming

   c. meditating

 Tell a family member something new you learned from this unit.

Name _____ Date _____

Vocabulary

Use with Student Book pages 270–271.

Key Words

tributaries
national parks
cliffs
sequoias
grove

A. **Choose the word that *best* fits each clue. Write the word.**

1. an area of land with one type of tree

_____

2. rivers that flow into larger rivers _____

3. large trees that grow in the Northwest _____

4. parks created by a country's government

_____

5. tall, steep faces of a mountain, often made of rock or ice

_____

B. **Choose the word that *best* completes each sentence. Write the word.**

6. The Missouri River and the Ohio River are

_____ of the Mississippi River.

7. _____ are believed to be the tallest trees in the world.

8. El Capitan and Devil's Tower are famous _____ in the United States.

9. Acadia, Yosemite, and Yellowstone are all

_____ .

C. Answer the questions.

10. Where might you find **cliffs**?

_____

11. What kinds of trees might you find in a **grove**?

_____

12. Why do people like visiting our **national parks**?

_____

13. What rivers are **tributaries** of larger rivers?

_____

14. Why is it important to protect the giant **sequoias**?

_____

Academic Words

D. Read each sentence. Write a new sentence using the underlined word.

15. The rug only covered a small <u>area</u> of the floor.

_____

16. The storm will affect the northern <u>region</u> of the country.

_____

 **Home-School Connection** Use each key word in a sentence. Share your sentences with a family member.

Name _____ Date _____

Reader's Companion

Use with Student Book pages 272–275.

Yosemite National Park

The U.S. government stepped in to help. In 1890, the area became known as Yosemite National Park. Rules make sure the land is preserved for people to enjoy now and in the future. More than three million people visit the park each year.

Yosemite Valley is a popular destination for visitors. It has cliffs and rock forms. Many guests spend time gazing at its waterfalls. Yosemite Valley is open all year. People often travel to the valley by car.

Yosemite National Park is also famous for its trees. Giant sequoias seem to reach the sky. The biggest group of giant sequoias is found in Mariposa Grove. Between November and March, the road to Mariposa Grove is closed to cars because of snow. Can you think of other ways to reach the grove? You can hike or ski!

Use What You Know

List three things you might find in a national park.

1. _____

2. _____

3. _____

Genre

Underline the words in the passage that make you think this is part of a travel article.

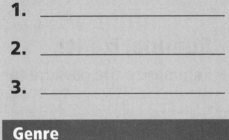

Reading Strategy

What connections from the article can you make to your own life?

_____

_____

_____

_____

Use the Strategy

How did making connections between your own life and the selection help you understand it?

_____

_____

_____

Summarize It!

Summarize the passage for a partner.

_____

_____

_____

_____

Reader's Response

Why is it important for the U.S. government to create national parks?

_____

_____

_____

 **Summarize the passage for a family member.**

Name _____ Date _____

Phonics: Words with *v* and *w*

Use with Student Book page 276.

Read each clue. Write the word that matches the clue. Then take turns saying the words aloud with a partner.

| vacation | van | vegetables | vertical | vowels |
| warm | wilderness | winter | wolf | worry |

1. animal related to a dog _____

2. *a, e, i, o,* and *u* are these _____

3. a small truck _____

4. a cold season _____

5. corn and lettuce _____

6. neither cold nor hot _____

7. time away from home or work _____

8. where the deer and the antelope live _____

9. straight up and down _____

10. think a lot about something _____

Find five words that begin with the letters *v* or *w*.
Practice saying them correctly with a family member.

Comprehension: Connect Text to Self

Use with Student Book pages 278–279.

Read each passage. Write how you might make a connection between each passage and your own life.

A Trip to the Museum

We have been learning about dinosaurs in school. My teacher decided to take the class to the museum to see the new dinosaur exhibit. The museum had many dinosaur bones under glass for us to look at. Scientists put together some models of dinosaur skeletons, so we could see how big the dinosaurs actually were in real life. They were huge! Some of the skeletons looked really mean. I wouldn't want to have lived in the time of the dinosaurs!

1. _____

_____

The New Book

Mrs. Milton reads to us every day after recess. She held up a new book today. The book had a large picture of the Moon on it. Laura raised her hand. "Is that the Moon?" she asked. "Yes," Mrs. Milton said. "This book is about the first people who landed on the Moon. I was your age when I saw it on TV in 1969. What do you think it's like on the Moon?" The class was excited. This is going to be a cool book!

2. _____

_____

 **Have a family member read or tell you a story. The family member can use his or her own language. Talk about how the story connects to your own life.**

Name _____ Date _____

Grammar: Four Types of Sentences

Use with Student Book page 280.

> **Declarative** sentences state something. **Interrogative** sentences ask questions. **Exclamatory** sentences express strong feelings. **Imperative** sentences tell someone to do (or not do) something.

Read each sentence. Write whether it is a declarative, interrogative, exclamatory, or imperative sentence. The first one is done for you.

1. Many people visit Yosemite National Park. _____declarative_____

2. This is a great idea! _____

3. Who makes sure the animals are okay? _____

4. The ranger will guide us through the park. _____

5. Don't walk across the grass! _____

6. Where do sequoias grow? _____

7. We found a nest in a tree. _____

8. Get down from there! _____

9. What is your favorite outdoor activity? _____

10. Come and visit our national parks! _____

Home-School Connection Write your own examples of each type of sentence. Share your sentences with a family member.

Spelling: Prefixes and Suffixes

Use with Student Book page 281.

Read each clue. Use the correct prefix or suffix from the chart to spell the word.

Prefixes	re	dis
Suffixes	ful	ness

1. to appear again

_____

2. noun using neat

_____

3. full of power   _____

4. make again   _____

5. to not like   _____

6. noun using great   _____

7. full of color   _____

8. to not connect   _____

 Write a journal entry using at least three words that have the prefixes and suffixes above.

_____

_____

_____

 Write two new words for each prefix and suffix. Share your words with a family member.

Name _____ Date _____

Vocabulary

Use with Student Book pages 282–283.

Copyright © by Pearson Education, Inc.

Key Words
environment
ecosystem
alpine
landslide
conservation
secluded
scenic

A. Choose the word that *best* completes each sentence. Write the word.

1. The land, water, and air in which people, plants,

and animals live is an _____ .

2. The protection of natural things is

_____ .

3. A place with beautiful views is _____ .

4. All of the plants and animals in a particular area is an

_____ .

5. The sudden fall of soil and rocks down the side of a mountain is

called a _____ .

6. Something in or related to high mountains is

_____ .

7. A place that is very quiet and private is _____ .

B. Find the key word in the row of letters. Write the word.

8. ghuoeghecosystemduvho _____

9. drvgbwenvironment _____

10. vunrnvscenicugouu _____

11. fvbrivblandslideeruvn _____

C. Answer the questions.

12. What are some **alpine** sports?

_____

13. Where might you have a **scenic** view?

_____

14. How can you protect the **environment**?

_____

15. Why is **conservation** work important?

_____

16. How might a **landslide** affect an **ecosystem**?

_____

17. Why would you want to visit a **secluded** area?

_____

Academic Words

D. Read each sentence. Write a new sentence using the underlined word.

18. Please give me a <u>specific</u> example of your problem.

_____

19. El Capitan and Yosemite Falls are some of the <u>features</u> of Yosemite National Park.

_____

Use each key word in a sentence. Share your sentences with a family member.

Name _____ Date _____

Reader's Companion

Use with Student Book pages 284–289.

How to Prepare for a Trip to Yosemite

Hi Jay,

What great news! You and your family will love Yosemite.

I did go there last year. But I've been to Yosemite many times. I only live a few hours from the park. My family and I go as often as we can.

I will tell you about the spots you really need to see. The first is Yosemite Valley. You will love the waterfalls and cliffs. Don't miss it! If you like giant sequoia trees, you have to go to Mariposa Grove. The best views are at Glacier Point. Long ago, a landslide shaped that part of the park.

Please tell your mom that fishing is allowed in the Merced River. Fishing does not disturb the park's ecosystem. There are some rules, but they are clearly posted. They tell where you can fish and the kinds of bait you can use. The trails are marked easy or hard. There are so many trails. Did you decide between renting a cabin or bringing your own tent?

Your friend,
Maria

Use What You Know

List three places Maria thinks Jay should see.

1. _____

2. _____

3. _____

Comprehension Check
MARK the TEXT

Underline what Maria told Jay about fishing in the Merced River.

Reading Strategy
MARK the TEXT

How does Maria feel about Yosemite? Circle the text where you found your answer.

_____

_____

_____

143

Use the Strategy

How did drawing conclusions help you understand the passage?

_____

_____

_____

Summarize It!

Summarize the passage for a partner.

_____

_____

_____

_____

Reader's Response

What would you like to see and do in Yosemite National Park?

_____

_____

_____

Summarize the passage for a family member.

Name _____ Date _____

Phonics: Variant Vowel *oo*

Use with Student Book page 290.

Read each sentence. Underline the *oo* words that have the sound you hear in *took*. Draw a box around the *oo* words that have the sound you hear in *too*. The first one is done for you.

1. Have people ever <u>stood</u> on the ⬚Moon⬚?

2. I learned how to cook in school.

3. The wind took the roof off our house.

4. Bamboo and oak are two kinds of wood.

5. A cool breeze feels good on a hot day!

6. The book was full of Mother Goose rhymes.

7. There is a zoo in the neighborhood.

8. Here's a cool picture of the fish I didn't hook.

9. Don't be gloomy. Things will look better tomorrow.

10. My sister took the shampoo!

11. Don't forget to bring your notebook to our classroom.

12. My little sister lost her book in my bedroom.

Think of five more words with variant sound /oo/. Show your words to a family member.

Comprehension: Draw Conclusions

Use with Student Book pages 292–293.

Read the passage. Answer the questions.

The View

"Look over there," said Marilee. "You can see the whole town!" Buddy quickly turned his head. He could see Main Street and their school. "Look over there," said Buddy, as the wind blew off his baseball cap. "You can see the little island where we go camping every summer." Marilee and Buddy were having a great time. "Too bad we have to go soon," said Marilee. Buddy smiled. "I know," he said. "Mom wants us home at five o'clock."

1. Where are Marilee and Buddy?
   _____ **a.** in an airplane
   _____ **b.** on the side of a hill
   _____ **c.** in their backyard

2. Explain why you chose your answer. Explain why you didn't choose the other two answers.

_____

_____

_____

3. Do Marilee and Buddy want to go home? Why or why not?

_____

_____

Have a family member read or tell you a story. The family member can use his or her own language. Talk about what conclusions you can draw from the story.

Name _____ Date _____

Grammar: Active and Passive Voice

Use with Student Book page 294.

A. Write whether the following sentences are written in the active voice or in the passive voice.

1. My family camped in Yosemite. _____

2. The camper was driven by my Aunt Barb. _____

3. Our tent was knocked over by the wind. _____

4. The wind knocked over our tent. _____

B. Write new sentences, changing them from the passive voice to the active voice.

5. The balloons for the party were brought by Jane.

_____

6. New tracksuits have been provided by the school.

_____

7. The apple trees were watered every week by her neighbor.

_____

8. The dog was walked by me.

_____

Find five sentences in a newspaper or magazine article. Write whether each sentence is in active or passive voice. Share your examples with a family member.

Spelling:

Checking Your Spelling

Use with Student Book page 295.

Write the correct word to complete each sentence.

1. Andy wanted an apple,

_____ .
        (to   too   two)

2. _____ the best player on the team.
        (Your   You're)

3. I would like to pass my art _____ .
                                    (coarse   course)

4. I _____ your invitation to the party.
        (accept   except)

5. I put my _____ on when I get dressed.
                (close   clothes)

6. The head of the school is the _____ .
                                      (principle   principal)

 Write a paragraph using at least three words that can be mistaken for other words.

_____

_____

 **Find five more words that you confuse with other words. Look up each word in the dictionary and use it in a sentence. Show your work to a family member.**

Name _____ Date _____

Vocabulary

Use with Student Book pages 296–297.

Key Words

cascade
meadow
peak
ascend
forest
valley

A. Choose the word that *best* fits each definition. Write the word.

1. an area of lower land between two

hills or mountains _____

2. a very large number of trees covering

a large area of land _____

3. to move to the top of something; to go up

_____

4. a field with wild grass or flowers _____

5. the pointed top of a mountain _____

6. a steep, usually small, waterfall _____

B. Choose the word that *best* matches the meaning of the underlined words. Write the word.

7. Many different animals live in the <u>wooded area</u>.

_____

8. We hoped to <u>make our way to the top of</u> the steep cliff.

_____

9. Snow covered the <u>highest point</u> of the mountain.

_____

C. Answer the questions.

10. When does water **cascade** heavily down a hill?

_____

11. What do climbers use to **ascend** a cliff?

_____

12. What animals and plants might you find in a **forest**?

_____

13. How would you describe a **meadow**?

_____

14. Why might a mountain **peak** be covered in snow during the summer?

_____

15. Where might you find a **valley**?

_____

Academic Words

D. Read each sentence. Write a new sentence using the underlined word.

16. Jay wanted Maria to <u>comment</u> on his scrapbook.

_____

17. Jay and Maria like to <u>correspond</u> by e-mail.

_____

 Use each key word in a sentence. Share your sentences with a family member.

Name _____ Date _____

Reader's Companion

Use with Student Book pages 298–301.

My Trip to Yosemite

August 7

On our first day, we drove to Glacier Point. Our goal was to ascend to the very top. We had a great view from there. We saw a huge waterfall. We could see Yosemite Valley at the bottom. There were so many trees in the valley! We saw Half Dome mountain. It looks like the top of a circle. We passed rock climbers on the way down. People from all over the world come to climb rocks in Yosemite. It looked fun but also a little scary!

Use What You Know

List three things you saw at a place you visited.

1. _____

2. _____

3. _____

Comprehension Check MARK the TEXT

What is the author describing? Underline the words that helped you find your answer.

_____

_____

_____

_____

Reading Strategy MARK the TEXT

Review the passage with a partner. Circle the words you would use to talk about the passage with a partner.

Use the Strategy

How did reviewing and retelling help you to understand the selection?

_____

_____

_____

Summarize It!

Summarize the passage for a partner.

_____

_____

_____

_____

Reader's Response

Would you like to go rock climbing? Why or why not?

_____

_____

_____

Summarize the passage for a family member.

Name _____   Date _____

Word Analysis: Greek and Latin Roots

Use with Student Book page 302.

Read each sentence. Write the Greek or Latin root that each underlined word comes from. The first one is done for you.

Latin Roots	Greek Roots
sub: under	*log*: speech
vac: to empty	*path*: feeling, suffering
cele: to honor	*scope*: to see
vis: to look	*phon*: sound

1. A <u>submarine</u> can travel deep below the sea.

   _____ sub _____

2. Air is <u>invisible</u>. _____

3. I felt a lot of <u>sympathy</u> for the sick kitten. _____

4. Did you hear the <u>telephone</u> ring? _____

5. The actors had a lot of <u>dialogue</u> to learn. _____

6. You can see Mars with a <u>telescope</u>. _____

7. We like to <u>celebrate</u> on holidays. _____

8. I <u>vacuum</u> the rug every morning to get it clean.

   _____

Find five more words with Greek or Latin roots. Show your words to a family member.

Comprehension: Review and Retell

Use with Student Book pages 304–305.

Read the passage. Answer the questions.

An Island Adventure

Dad and I were stuck on an island. The island was out in the middle of the bay, not far from our house. We had been fishing offshore. Suddenly, it started getting windy. The sail ripped. "Let's pull the boat to shore," said Dad. Together, we pulled our small sailboat onto the sand. We sat and waited. We waited a bit longer. "I'm sure someone will come and find us," said Dad. "Don't worry," I said. "I left Mom a note. I told her we would be fishing near the island." Dad started to laugh. "You're very smart, Chelsea!" Within an hour, we saw Mom racing to the shore in our little speedboat. We were glad to see her. She brought lunch!

1. Why did Chelsea and her dad have to bring their boat ashore?

_____

_____

2. Why wasn't Chelsea worried about being stuck on the beach?

_____

_____

3. Why were Chelsea and her dad happy to see Mom?

_____

_____

Have a family member read or tell you a story. The family member can use his or her own language. Retell the story to another family member.

Name _____ Date _____

Grammar: Articles

Use with Student Book page 306.

Complete each sentence with the missing articles *a*, *an*, or *the*. Some examples have more than one correct answer.

1. I took _____ bus to school.

2. Would you like _____ apple?

3. My father is _____ teacher.

4. _____ snow made the ground white.

5. We use articles when we speak English in _____ United States.

6. Jay is _____ student.

7. Maria had _____ idea for Jay's scrapbook.

8. Mrs. Jones turned off _____ light before leaving the classroom.

9. Can you give me _____ egg, please?

10. The teacher asked me to read _____ book for class.

11. Please turn off _____ television.

12. My parents bought _____ new car.

13. This story is about _____ elephant.

14. It is easy to find _____ hiking trail on the map.

Find a paragraph in a newspaper or magazine. Underline the articles you find. Show your work to a family member.

Spelling: Words That Are Difficult to Spell

Use with Student Book page 307.

Find the word in each sentence that is spelled incorrectly. Spell the word correctly.

SPELLING TIP

Keep a list in your notebook of words that you find hard to spell. Add to your list when you are reading or writing.

1. Every place on Earth is part of an ecosistem.

_____

2. Konservation work will save the

environment. _____

3. All of the smaller tributarys flowed into the big river.

_____

4. It took the climbers three days to reach the mowntain peak.

_____

5. We live on the edge of a national forrest. _____

6. We had fun rowwing our boat on the lake.

_____

 Write a paragraph using at least three words that you have had trouble spelling.

_____

_____

_____

 Write the dictionary definitions to three words you have trouble spelling. Show your work to a family member.

Name _____ Date _____

Review

Use with Student Book pages 264–307.

Answer the questions after reading Unit 6. You can go back and reread to help find the answers.

1. According to *Yosemite National Park*, how long have people lived in the Yosemite region? Circle the letter of the correct answer.

   a. 50 years   **c.** 100 years
   b. 8,000 years   **d.** 500 years

2. Why did the government create Yosemite National Park?

   _____

   _____

3. Why is it dangerous to climb El Capitan?

   _____

   _____

4. In *How to Prepare for a Trip to Yosemite*, which of the following is NOT one of the supplies to bring on a camping trip? Circle the letter of the correct answer.

   a. tent   **c.** mp3 player
   b. water   **d.** food

5. Why did Jay and his family go camping in the Poconos?

   _____

   _____

6. Complete the Sequence Chart. Explain three steps that Jay took to get ready for his trip to Yosemite.

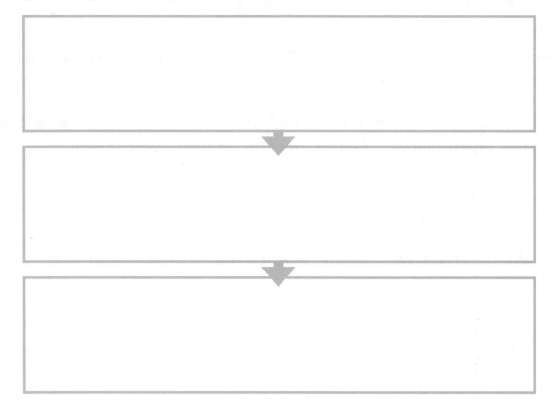

7. According to *My Trip to Yosemite*, which waterfall is the tallest waterfall in the United States? Circle the letter of the correct answer.

a. Niagara Falls **c.** Yosemite Falls

b. Vernal Falls **d.** Nevada Falls

8. Name three places Jay and his family visited.

_____

_____

9. What did Jay learn about Mirror Lake on his mule ride?

_____

_____

Home-School Connection Tell a family member something new you learned in this unit.

Copyright © by Pearson Education, Inc.